OFFICERS AND GENTLEMEN

Historic West Point In Photographs

OFFICERS AND GENTLEMEN

Historic West Point In Photographs

Jeffrey Simpson

Sleepy Hollow Press

Library of Congress Cataloging in Publication Data

Main entry under title:

Officers & gentlemen.

    Bibliography: p.
    Includes index.
    1. United States Military Academy—History and
Pictorial works. I. Simpson, Jeffrey. II. Title: Officers
and gentlemen.
U410.L3034   1982   355′.007′1173   82-16820
ISBN 0-912882-53-0

First Printing

For information, address the publisher:

SLEEPY HOLLOW PRESS
Sleepy Hollow Restorations, Inc.
150 White Plains Road
Tarrytown, New York 10591

Prepared for Sleepy Hollow Press by:
    Sachem Publishing Associates, Inc.
    Box 412
    Guilford, Connecticut 06437

Design by Kirchoff/Wohlberg, Inc.

Manufactured in the United States of America

A West Point cavalry formation (preceding page) *at the turn of the century presented the image of order, precision, and assurance associated with the Academy.*

CONTENTS

INTRODUCTION

Sylvanus Thayer, known as the Father of the Military Academy for his accomplishments as superintendent of West Point from 1817 until 1833, looks imposing and stern in a photograph taken shortly after the Civil War. Thayer was born in 1785, the son of a veteran of the recently concluded Revolutionary War. As an adult he was commissioned by the United States government to go to France to buy books and maps and to make studies of fortifications for the young military academy. He arrived in Paris on July 12, 1815, less than four weeks after the Battle of Waterloo. He knew Presidents James Madison, James Monroe, John Quincy Adams, and Andrew Jackson—who was the cause of his leaving West Point. After he left West Point on the downriver boat for New York one June evening in 1833, Thayer never returned to the institution that he had seen through its period of adolescence. Nonetheless, in 1870 he was elected the first president of the Association of Graduates. He died in 1872, when many of the leading military figures of the early 20th century were already young men.

These are facts of history. They are significant for our understanding of the past and, equally so, for our understanding of the present. But that understanding is intellectual. The immediate emotional impact of looking at Thayer's austere face and knowing who he was and what he did is something much more immediate and quite different. We experience the past when we look at old photographs in a way that is never possible from reading alone. When we look at the photograph of Thayer, there *is* the man who knew the mythic figures of Madison, Monroe, and Jackson. There *is* the man who saw the chaos following Napoleon's defeat. Looking at photographs we make a direct connection with history.

For this reason, exploring and presenting images that capture the lives and exploits of West Point officers is one of the richest ways of understanding our nation's past. West Point embodies the ideals and aspirations—and was sometimes caught squarely in the conflicts—of America's first two centuries. Photographs of old West Point and the campaigns and expeditions in which its graduates participated bring an essential part of American history to life.

The progress of the United States Military Academy at West Point was far from smooth in the early days and represents a conflict between idealism and practicality that has pervaded the United States from its beginnings. During the Revolutionary War there were few trained professional soldiers fighting for the colonies and, consequently, few officers with an understanding of military engineering. Such European volunteers as Thaddeus Kosciusko, Baron von Steuben, and the Marquis de Lafayette brought an understanding of troop movements and supply lines, drilling and marching, and defense works without which the war probably could not have been won. Nevertheless, once the Revolution was over, the United States cherished the conception of itself as a nation of independent citizens who would defend themselves with volunteer armies when necessary and wanted no association with such European pretensions as standing armies. George Washington, Alexander Hamilton, and the leading officers of the Revolutionary War understood how wrong this attitude was. Even if there were to be only volunteer militia armies in America, there had to be professional leaders trained to guide them. Alexander Hamilton wrote, "War, like most other things, is a science to be acquired and perfected by diligence." These men advocated the founding of a training school for officers. What swung the balance in favor of such a school—even in the eyes of Thomas Jefferson, who had originally opposed it—was the possibility that officers trained for military engineering could also build bridges, dams, harbors, and roads for the civilian population.

An institution that could produce trained military officers who also possessed then-rare engineering skills satisfied those who wanted a permanent officer corps and those who considered civilian projects paramount. With this dual mission in mind, the government established the Academy in 1802.

Although its graduates were prominent in civilian and military occupations within a few years, the Academy's worth was not generally conceded until after the Mexican War of 1846–1848. General in Chief Winfield Scott wrote some years later about that war: "I give it as my fixed opinion that but for our graduated cadets the war . . . probably would have lasted some four or five years . . . whereas in less than two campaigns, we conquered a great country and a peace, without the loss of a single battle or skirmish." Then, again, during the Civil War, when fifty-five out of the sixty major battles of the war were commanded on both sides by West Point graduates, there were serious questions about an institution that would breed such accomplished traitors (as the Northern half of the nation viewed the Southerners).

With the nation reunited by the North's victory, West Point's value was confirmed for the public. Then the dangers came more from within than without. But, again, those dangers were similar to the problems of the nation at large. In an age of burgeoning industrialism and the decline of the agrarian ideals on which the nation had been founded, West Point's complacency was no more or less smug than that of civilian institutions and population. At West Point a relaxing into the materialism and comfort of the moment threatened the reputation of one of the best military and engineering schools in the world.

With the campaigns of the frontier, the Spanish-American War, and the advent of World War I, America continued to grow and gleam as the image of the Promised Land, and West Point continued to graduate men of character, diversity, and military genius. In balance, despite social inequities in the nation at large and a certain failure to meet new challenges head on at West Point, both the country and the school fulfilled their early promises.

With the advent of Douglas MacArthur as superintendent in 1919, sweeping reforms were instituted that would correct Brigadier General MacArthur's exaggerated but heartfelt cry, "How much longer are we going to go on preparing for the War of 1812?" America had lost its innocence in World War I on the battlefields of France. West Point would lose its innocence under General MacArthur's stern but realistic vision of the needs of the modern world.

The end of the World War I era signaled the end of an era for the Academy, marked by the departure of MacArthur from West Point in 1922. During its first one hundred and twenty years, the Academy had experienced tremendous growth and change; its graduates had been commanders in two of the greatest conflicts the world had known and had distinguished themselves in several other major wars. In 1922, following what the world thought was "the war to end all wars," a period of consolidation and reevaluation began. Neither West Point nor the nation could know that ahead lay the global campaigns of World War II and the more localized conflicts in Korea and Vietnam.

Parallel in their problems and their promise, the Academy and the United States indeed became part of a "new world"—new beyond anything the first European explorers could possibly have imagined. Because of this parallel development and because of the immediacy and intimacy the photographic image brings to history, the privilege of compiling a photographic history of early West Point has been great and the value of publishing photographs from the Academy archives is incalculable. Superintendent Thayer, regarding us across more than a century with his chilly but honorable eye, offers one of many images of an American ideal.

The remains of Fort Clinton (right), a post used during the Revolutionary War, were long ignored after West Point was founded.

THE EARLY YEARS

Robert E. Lee never received a single demerit in his four years as a cadet; Ulysses S. Grant's one moment of glory as a cadet, on the other hand, was a feat of horsemanship, leaping over a pole three times in succession on a stallion called York; William Tecumseh Sherman was thought to be the best in his class at making midnight suppers of stolen chicken and potatoes roasted in the fireplace; George Armstrong Custer was nicknamed "Fanny" because of his long gold curls.

They were college boys, good or lazy, resourceful or vain. They were also cadets at the United States Military Academy, however, and the tempering process of those four years of training made them soldiers. Their personalities and the traits of thousands of others who graduated after West Point's founding in 1802—tacticians, strategists, engineers, and combat leaders—became part of a new nation's developing history. Lee remained a gentleman to the end, a man who commanded as much by his personal magnetism as by his tactical skills; Grant met crises with brilliant precision and audacity. Sherman's ruthlessness was equaled only by his resourcefulness; applying them together he developed the modern concept of total war. Custer's curls became a symbol of a last despairing gesture by American natives against unstoppable progress.

The integration of the personal into the common social good has always been one goal of education. At West Point that social good became identified with the national image. West Point cadets were educated to build—literally in the vast engineering works done by its early graduates—to assert the nation's rights, and then to defend the national security.

At the very beginning, in the nearly twenty years between the end of the American Revolution in 1783 and the passing of a bill by Congress in March 1802 charging that a new Corps of Engineers

In 1847, during the Mexican War, a sketch showed the library (center), Old Chapel (right), and Old Academic Building (far right). All were built of local granite, but while the chapel was Classical Revival, the library was in Superintendent Delafield's English Tudor style.

Academy Buildings, W.P.

"shall be stationed at West Point . . . and shall constitute a military academy," there was considerable opposition to the idea of a military school. Following imagined ideals of ancient Rome and Greece, which they thought they were reviving, many Americans distrusted the idea of a permanent professional army. There had been considerable opposition to the Society of the Cincinnati, an organization of Revolutionary War officers (with hereditary membership) on the grounds that it would lead to a hereditary aristocracy. Similarly, the notion of a standing army, instead of a militia composed of citizens who would rally as needed, was feared as feudal and undemocratic. But in fact, the Revolution could not have been won without the assistance of trained European soldiers who had come to the colonists' aid: the Marquis de Lafayette, who brought blankets, food supplies, and uniforms; Thaddeus Kosciusko, who designed forts and defense works; and Baron von Steuben, who drew up a manual of arms and taught the men how to drill, march, and maneuver. These Europeans aided the colonial cause and helped to convert colonial volunteers into soldiers who could hold their own against the superbly trained British. Nevertheless, once the war had been won, the need for trained soldiers went unrecognized, and the Army shrank to a few hundred men. Popular sentiment was strongly against the Army growing much larger or being directed by professionals.

Military leaders of the Revolution knew better. "I cannot conclude without repeating the necessity of the proposed institution [for military training] unless we intend to let the Science [of War] become extinct, and to depend entirely upon the Foreigners for their friendly aid," wrote Washington not long after the Revolution, and Alexander Hamilton noted, "War, like most other things is a science to be acquired and perfected by diligence . . ." In 1790, General Henry Knox, Secretary of War, who had declared early in the Revolution that "as the army now stands, it is merely a receptacle for ragamuffins," officially recommended the establishment of a military academy. At intervals over the last decade of the 18th century Washington and others again and again urged the need for a military school, but it was not until there was a threat of war with the French in 1798 and response of the local militias to

a national call to arms was woefully inadequate that the proposal gained significant Congressional support. In 1799, Alexander Hamilton drafted a plan for a complete military education, saying: "No sentiment is more just than this, that in proportion as the circumstances and policy of a country forbid a large military establishment, it is important that as much perfection as possible should be given to that which may at any time exist."

Thomas Jefferson, who had originally opposed the idea, was wooed by the image of the academy's also being a school for scientific training to be used in civilian life. He also came around to seeing the need for a corps of professionally trained officers and proposed the establishment of a military academy. On March 16, 1802, with the passage of the Military Peace Establishment Act, the Congress enacted the President's recommendations.

The European Heritage

The precedent that the new Academy would draw on, the idea that army officers required special training beyond riding and drilling, was a rather recent development in the age-old history of combat. It was only in the 18th century, in response to the possibilities of newly refined artillery and engineering practices, that the European military schools had been established. Traditionally, the aristocracy had completely reserved the leadership of the armies for themselves, and commissions as officers were bought for younger sons of noble families. Armies were made up of professional mercenaries who could not make a living any other way and who were directed—and even bought and sold—at the will of their princely leaders. With increasingly sophisticated artillery and the engineering of fortifications, after the Renaissance, however, officers had to be found who were mathematicians and engineers. Mastery of these subjects offered a road for advancement to the bourgeoisie, for the largely undereducated aristocrats preferred to keep the leadership of the infantry and cavalry for themselves.

In France under Louis XIV the first systematic attempt to educate an officer corps occurred, but this first effort was directed toward the sons of noble families, who refused to accept the discipline of a cadet corps, and the school was disbanded. A second

In 1841, Charles Dickens wrote of West Point, "It could not stand on more appropriate ground, and any ground more beautiful can hardly be."

school was suggested by the Paris brothers, financiers who were bankers to Louis XV and one of whom may have been the unacknowledged father of Madame de Pompadour. This École Militaire was supported at court by Madame de Pompadour; and, accordingly, Louis XV commissioned it in 1751. It was attended by cadets from provincial military schools, including the young Napoleon Bonaparte. During the French Revolution it would be named the École de Mars, and afterwards, under Napoleon, as the École Polytechnique it became one of the greatest engineering schools in the world.

In England, King George II had also recognized the need for trained personnel to deal with new developments in military science, developments that officers who had bought their commissions and resisted innovation were not equipped to do. The result was the Royal Military Academy at Woolwich, founded in 1741. Prussia, despite its respected reputation for military efficiency under Frederick the Great, had no place in its social or military structure for bourgeois artillerists, so there was no training school until after a defeat by Napoleon demonstrated its necessity.

13

One of the most successful defensive feats during the Revolution had been the stretching of a massive chain across the Hudson at West Point to prevent the British from sailing up the river and dividing the colonies. Remnants of the chain such as the links displayed at West Point (above), were cherished as Revolutionary War relics.

Trophies (left) captured in wars from the American Revolution to the Spanish-American War were enshrined at West Point when this turn of the century photograph was taken.

15

The Choice of West Point

When Thomas Jefferson supported the establishment of the United States Military Academy, his reasoning in part relied on the tradition of a general scientific education that the European schools promoted. If the American aim was to have as small a standing army as possible, then that army should be as well trained as possible (as Hamilton had pointed out) so it could lead citizen soldiers most efficiently in an emergency. When there was no emergency, the officers informed in the science of war could implement the same sciences in peacetime. Engineers who could build earthworks and pontoon bridges for armies could also build harbors and bridges for trade and transportation. More subjectively, Jefferson hoped that men from good Republican stock would go to such an academy and rise to positions of leadership, thereby lessening Federalist influence in the Army.

With all of the dissension about whether there was to be a military academy or not, however, there had never been any serious doubt about where it should be established. West Point, a plateau jutting out into the Hudson River fifty miles north of New York harbor, had been called "the key to the Continent" by Washington during the Revolution. It was

fortified early in the war, and it was at West Point that a gigantic chain was stretched across the river to prevent the British from sailing up and effectively cutting off New England from the rest of the colonies. West Point's fortifications were designed by Thaddeus Kosciuszko, the best engineer among the foreign volunteers in the Revolution, and it was West Point that the arch-traitor Benedict Arnold tried to betray to the British for £20,000 and a commission in the British Army. Washington and the Continental Army waited near West Point from 1782 until the formal close of the war and the British withdrawal from New York City in 1783. After the war a garrison was maintained at West Point, and it was

there that the cannons and other trophies from the battles of Saratoga, Stony Point, and Yorktown were stored, thus indicating that even at that date West Point held a special place in the imagination of the new republic.

In 1790, West Point became a permanent military post of the United States Army, and the Corps of Artillerists and Engineers was stationed there. In 1802, when that corps was divided and the new Corps of Engineers was charged by Congress to direct a military academy, the obvious choice of a site was West Point.

From the heights, 190 feet above the river, artillery batteries could command traffic on the Hudson. George Washington, appreciating West Point's strategic importance, called it the "key to the continent."

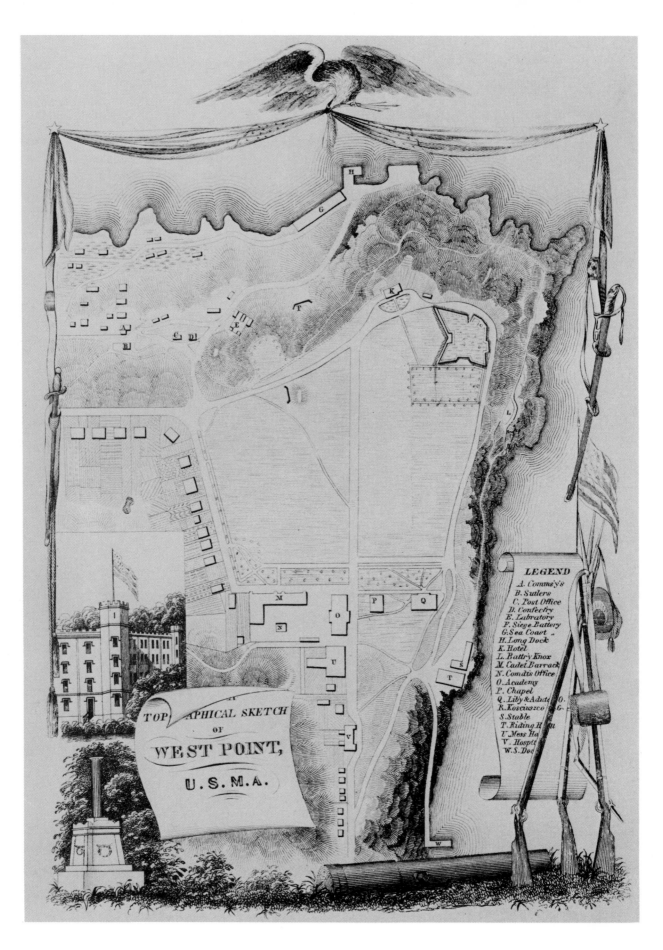

TOPOGRAPHICAL SKETCH OF WEST POINT, U.S.M.A.

LEGEND
A. Comms'y's
B. Sutlers
C. Post Office
D. Confect'ry
E. Labratory
F. Siege Battery
G. Sea Coast
H. Long Dock
K. Hotel
L. Batt'ry Knox
M. Cadet Barrack
N. Comd'ts Office
O. Academy
P. Chapel
Q. Liby & Adute O.
R. Koscuszco's G.
S. Stable
T. Riding Hall
U. Mess Hall
V. Hospt'l
W. S. Dock

The First Years

The military academy was proclaimed into existence on March 16, 1802, but for the next fifteen years it would limp along with its survival a matter of almost daily doubt. The first directive had been that the Chief Engineer of the Corps of Engineers was to be the Superintendent of the Academy, which was to consist of seven officers and ten cadets. Jonathan Williams, the first superintendent, had been appointed chief engineer because of his knowledge of science and his reputation as a man of practical learning. He was a nephew of Benjamin Franklin, with a similarly inquiring mind. His interests and qualifications led Williams to appoint a good faculty for the Academy and to appreciate its unique—although at this time theoretical—function. He avoided the traditional academic curriculum of the classics and instead emphasized mathematics, the physical sciences, French—in which the foremost military instruction of the day was being written—and drawing, which could be applied to military engineering as drafting.

One of the strongest differences between a classical education as it had evolved in European universities and the curricula of New World colleges was that European universities essentially functioned as repositories of knowledge and sophisticated finishing schools in which gentlemen were taught how to cultivate their minds and use their leisure. The New World, on the other hand, had need of professional men in every backwoods community. There was a chronic shortage of doctors, lawyers, ministers, and teachers. New World colleges had to provide these; they had to be pre-professional training schools. West Point, as Jonathan Williams set it up, fell in this category with a slight difference: the Army needed officers and that was what the Academy would provide.

The narrow boundaries and limited physical plant of 19th century West Point, isolated on its promontory, are suggested in this map (left) *made at the time of the Civil War.*

Fort Putnam (below), *one of the Revolutionary War fortifications that had defended West Point, was maintained with artillery guns well into the 19th century.*

Fed on a diet of boiled potatoes, stringy meat, bread, and coffee, cadets were always hungry. Extra food, known in cadet slang as "hash," was often cooked over a fire in the barracks in a typical student gesture of rebellion against official rules, as this 19th century sketch suggests.

One tacit function shared by most other American colleges and the military academy was to educate men morally. Most universities had ties to some particular Protestant denomination, and courses in moral philosophy figured prominently. The military academy for the most part avoided this emphasis and replaced the Greek and Latin needed by doctors and lawyers with French and physics.

Williams was superintendent from 1802 until 1812 (with a two year absence caused by a disagreement with the War Department), and his academic plan for the Academy was sound. The problems, however, were overwhelming. Because he was also chief engineer, Williams could devote only a little time to the Academy, and he was rarely there. There were few requirements for entering—until 1810 any man who wanted to could register for courses—and the cadets included a twelve-year-old boy, a man with one arm, and a married man who brought his wife. The buildings were inadequate, and after 1803, when all non-engineering personnel were transferred to other posts, West Point was not only somewhat derelict but also nearly empty. The biggest problem was that despite President Jefferson's support Congress did not care about the Academy, and many members were still actively hostile to it.

The Academy reached its nadir at the start of the War of 1812, when most of the officers on the faculty were called up for mobilization along with the graduating cadets, leaving in attendance only one cadet and one officer with the civilian faculty. At the same time, however, a reorganization was implemented that laid foundations for the future Academy. Jonathan Williams had retired from the Army in 1812, and he was replaced as chief engineer by Colonel Joseph Swift, who, in due course, became superintendent. Swift had been the Academy's first graduate in 1802, and he was one of an exceptional handful of these early graduates who devoted enor-

Jonathan Williams, the Army's chief engineer and the first superintendent of West Point (1802–1803 and 1805–1812), established the base for a good academic program although few regulations governed the Academy.

Colonel Joseph Swift, the Academy's first graduate, became its second superintendent in 1812. He imposed cohesiveness on West Point but was often absent on his duties as chief engineer.

mous energy and intelligence to their infant alma mater. Swift got Congress to agree to a raising of the number of cadets to 250 (although the previous quotas of 50 and 156 had never been filled); he enlarged the faculty, including hiring the first professor of engineering, and he organized the cadets into a Corps of Cadets, divided into companies. Unfortunately, Swift's plans were only partially put into effect because of the war, but at the same time President James Madison in 1813 encouraged the admission of as many cadets as possible, young men who could be quickly trained for junior commissions to help in the war. Thus, during Swift's administration West Point was saved because it was needed, additional useful ground rules were established, and its value was tacitly recognized in Washington.

Alden Partridge

Because Joseph Swift, as chief engineer, was so entirely occupied with the progress of the war, his duties at the Academy were carried out by Captain Alden Partridge, the senior member of the faculty, who had graduated from the Academy in 1806. Partridge, devoted and difficult, was acting superintendent and then superintendent until 1817. As earlier superintendents had laid the grounds for the academic policies and general direction of the Academy, so Partridge would contribute largely to the actual look and structure of the place. One of his first acts was to institute a strict regime of military discipline. While a cadet, he wrote "[I] was drilled but twice after entering the Academy before I was required to instruct cadets in the duties of the company. The consequence was that I and other cadets acquired a smattering of elementary duty, partly right, partly wrong." Partridge dispelled the informal militia atmosphere forever, instituting a program of rigid drills and graduated, increasingly severe punishments to cover every infraction. He regimented the cadets' day as totally and severely as he did their movements, ranging from roll call and inspection before breakfast at seven o'clock to supper, a study period, and bed. Partridge established the invaluable graduation requirements that insured that the young lieutenants coming out of the Academy would truly be educated officers and gentlemen, not just civilians with a little drill practice brushed on for the purpose of duty in a current

Alden Partridge (Class of 1806), the first superintendent who was not also the Army's chief engineer, was an unpopular autocrat, but he made very real contributions of scheduling and discipline.

campaign. He built two new gray stone barracks that were badly needed and that set the tone for West Point's physical appearance. Lastly, one of his most visible legacies is the cadet uniform. "The long gray line" owes its look to Alden Partridge, who adapted the cadet uniform from those worn by General Winfield Scott's troops at the Battle of Chippewa in 1814.

Unfortunately, Partridge, who was known as "Old Pewter" or just plain "Old Pewt" to the cadets because of his inflexibly metallic personality, was touchy, vain, and suspicious. He thought that no one could do anything unless he was involved, while at the same time he resented the burdens thrust upon him. He was particularly suspicious of the faculty and indeed hounded them until they went to Colonel Swift, Partridge's predecessor and his direct superior as chief engineer. (The superintendency had been separated from the position of chief engineer in 1815). Swift initiated court martial proceedings against Partridge. When President James Monroe visited West Point in June 1817 with Colonel Swift to inspect conditions for himself, he found that discipline and morale had completely deteriorated.

When Partridge refused to be replaced, he was convicted of disobedience to orders and cashiered with a recommendation for clemency by President Monroe in view of his substantial work at the Academy. He left, bitter and vowing retribution. The Academy was turned over to Sylvanus Thayer, whose educational and organizational genius was matched by a personality in which austerity inspired confidence as much as Partridge's rigid nature had offended. It was Thayer who would finally establish the Academy as a national institution and earn himself the title "Father of the United States Military Academy."

Sylvanus Thayer

Thayer, it has been said, made West Point one of the great scientific institutions of the New World and a model for other colleges. Although there were soon competitors—Partridge established what became Norwich University in 1819 and Rensselaer Polytechnic Institute was founded in 1824—West Point was for awhile the only college in the country with an engineering course, and it remained one of

Sylvanus Thayer, when he was photographed in the 1860s, had not seen West Point for thirty years. While superintendent (1817–1833), he hired a respected faculty and created the cadet ranking system.

Merit it's own Reward
or
The best man leads off the Squad.

the best up to the Civil War. Thayer's achievement was to build on the academic structure set up by his predecessors, to bring the Academy favorably into the public eye, and to initiate a ranking system whereby each cadet was graded daily on his class recitations and general behavior and accumulated points or demerits accordingly. The cadets at the bottom of the class went into the infantry, while those in the top portions went into the Engineering and Artillery Corps, thus initiating West Point's reputation for graduating accomplished tacticians.

Thayer's personality was the sort that attracts respect and legends without compromising one whit its own dignity. He was known to be strict but fair, in the tradition of the best teachers. When he met a cadet who had sneaked away without permission at a dinner party on the Hudson's eastern shore, Thayer was polite to the sweating lad, courteously exchanged toasts with him at dinner, and then reprimanded the young man's cadet leader on his return for not noticing the absence. The cadet himself never heard another word about the incident. Thayer kept up his reputation for omniscience by having daily reports about each cadet posted inside the pigeonholes of his desk so that when a cadet came to him with a problem Thayer seemed— as indeed he was—intimately acquainted with the daily details of post life. Cadets informed about their indebtedness to the penny when asking for an advance on their pay were staggered at Thayer's insight.

Thayer had been a farmer's son from Braintree, Massachusetts, the nest of the Adamses whose disciplined, slightly chilly contributions to the national good exceeded even his own, and he had graduated in the class of 1808 from the Academy after taking a degree from Dartmouth. He served as a professor of mathematics at the Academy from 1810 to 1812

and then as an engineering officer during the War of 1812. In 1815, Thayer asked for a leave of absence to travel to Europe and study French military tactics at first hand. President Madison and Secretary of War James Monroe decided that Thayer should go officially and study the methods of the École Polytechnique, as well as buying books and maps for West Point. The École Polytechnique, the heir of Louis XV's École Militaire, had become the greatest academic beneficiary of Napoleon's military genius and a breeding ground for his officers. Thayer stayed a year, absorbing the military and civil engineering curricula, and returned with a thousand volumes on tactics, engineering, mathematics, and the humanities, as well as detailed maps of Europe and the Napoleonic campaigns. This collection was a rich resource for the cadets and faculty and became the nucleus of the Academy's library.

With the fervor of one who had found his vocation, he declared about his appointment as superintendent of the Academy in 1817: "I had a solemn duty to perform and was determined to perform it whatever were the personal consequences to myself."

In 1816, just before Thayer had been made superintendent, the Secretary of War had established the Board of Visitors, whose members would be "five gentlemen versed in military and other science" who would attend the Academy's twice yearly examinations and verbally examine the cadets along with the Academic Board, which was composed of the faculty. The Board of Visitors proved to be a valuable liaison between the superintendent and the outside world. Over the years it was composed of government figures, retired generals, and distinguished alumni.

In addition to establishing the ranking system for cadets and collecting a distinguished faculty (the one that was there when he arrived although not undistinguished was almost completely demoralized by Partridge's constant meddling in their work), Thayer saw that the Academy was recognized as unique and valuable. He made the cadets visible models of trim military style with such grassroots publicity as marches to Boston and Philadelphia during the three-month summer camp period when the cadets were actually instructed about life in the field. And he also kept in touch with the

James Abbott McNeill Whistler, who became one of America's foremost painters, was a predictably unsuitable cadet at West Point, excelling only in drawing class. His satiric sketches of cadet life (left) captured early cadet life.

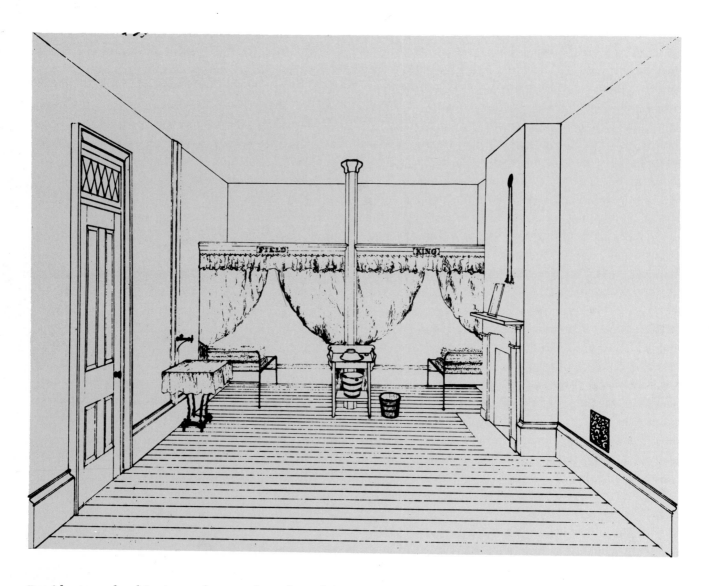

Cadet barracks life, as this 1860 drawing shows, was Spartan in the extreme, despite curtained alcoves. Each man rolled up his bedding when he rose at 5:30 A.M., turned over his washbowl after using it, and emptied his "slop bucket," which stood beneath the washstand.

Presidents and cabinet members under whom he served, with such beneficial results as President Andrew Jackson declaring in his first message to the nation in 1829 that "I recommend to your fostering care, as one of our safest means of national defense, the Military Academy . . ."

Unfortunately, along with a raised public consciousness of the Academy came an increased sense of proprietorship, particularly from political figures who had appointed cadets to the school. Cadets who had been suspended or dismissed could always be reinstated by direct application to the President, and in those democratic days when any citizen could walk into the White House (which after all the citizens owned) and shake the President's hand, such direct application was all too often a reality. There were still repeated bills introduced in Congress to abolish the Academy, the supporters of the bills reasoning that there was no war and if there was no need for a citizen's army, there was no need for officers. One bill was introduced in 1830 by Davy Crockett, the self-sufficient frontiersman and representative from Tennessee. When President Jackson, a frontier democrat who had campaigned on a platform that deplored the frills of the Eastern establishment, had trouble with Thayer's discipline of his own two nephews at West Point, his approval of the Academy turned decidedly tepid. Jackson believed that the Academy was a national asset and never withdrew his support, but he undermined Thayer's dismissals of cadets a number of times. Finally, in 1832, when President Jackson reinstated Cadet Ariel Norris, who had been dismissed for setting up a hickory pole (Jackson's campaign symbol) in front of the superintendent's house, Thayer sent in his resignation. The faculty was appalled, but Thayer would allow no active demonstrations that appeared disloyal to the administration, and one evening in June 1833, after taking a stroll down to the dock with faculty friends and officers, he stepped onto the steamboat bound for New York and never—in a life that lasted another thirty-nine years—saw West Point again.

The Legacy of Thayer

One of Thayer's most evident legacies at the time was a stellar faculty. He hired Claude Crozet, a graduate of the École Polytechnique and the author of two important texts on geometry, to teach engineering; Charles Davies, Class of 1815, was appointed to teach mathematics and produced a number of important texts used throughout the United States. Claudius Beard, the author of several textbooks on learning French, was already at West Point to teach that language so essential in military matters at the time. In 1830, Thayer hired Dennis Hart Mahan, Class of 1822, as professor of engineering and the art of war. William Bartlett, Class of 1826, who became a professor of natural philosophy (today known as physics) and one of the country's foremost astronomers, and Albert Church, who succeeded Davies as a professor of mathematics, also helped to make West Point the greatest scientific institution in America for the first half of the 19th century. These men, because of enormous natural intelligence, because they were creating a

Dennis Hart Mahan, Class of 1824, served as a professor of engineering from 1830 until his death in 1871. His own textbooks included the influential Outpost, *used by commanders on both sides during the Civil War. Mahan emphasized that speed and the occupation of key points were more important than destruction of enemy forces.*

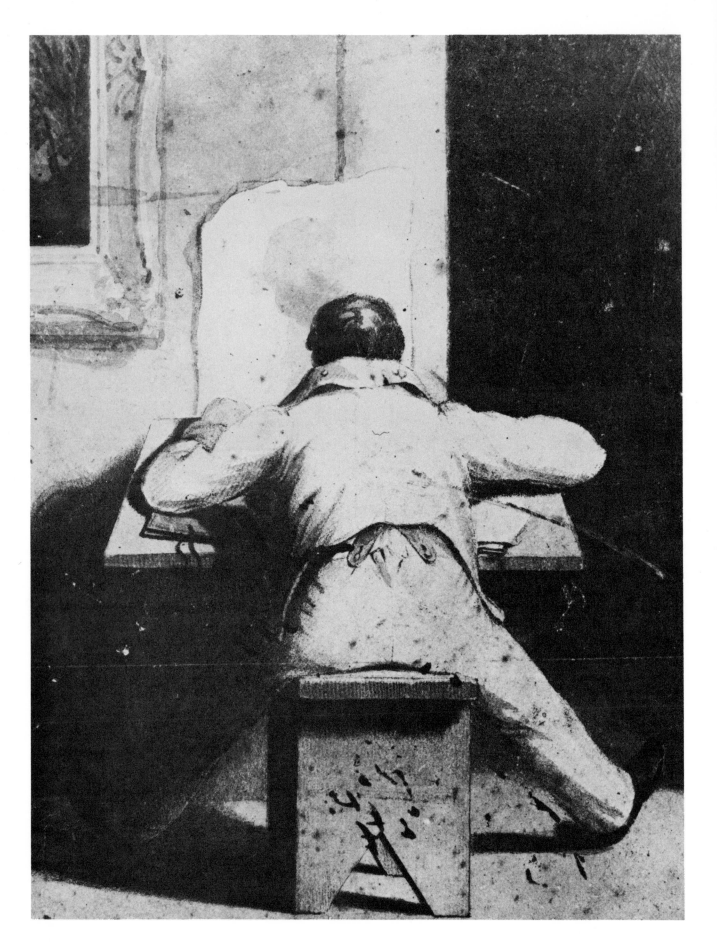

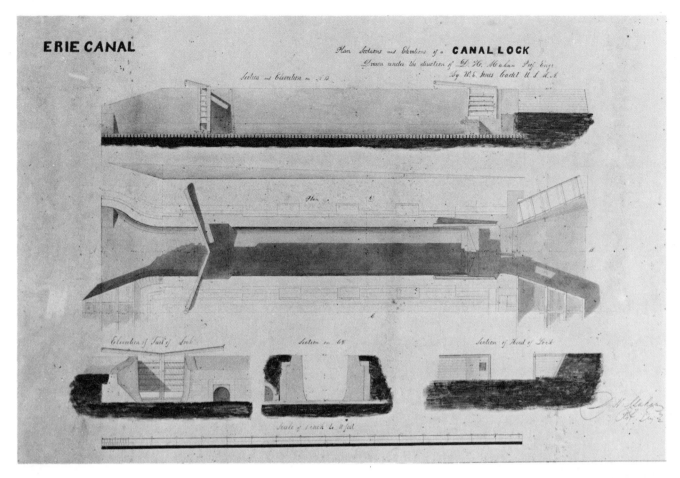

ERIE CANAL

A cadet's study drawings of the Erie Canal lock system (above), *part of engineering training, were submitted to Professor Mahan.*

A cadet, sprawled across a drawing board in the 1830s (left), *learns drafting.*

school of a sort that had never before existed and had to write their own texts, and because of their length of tenure—most of them stayed at West Point for more than forty years until well after the Civil War—formed an extraordinary constellation of talent. They established the academic character of the school and influenced the state of engineering and campaign strategy all through 19th century America. Dennis Mahan's work and influence are emblematic of the intellectual influence of West Point during this era.

Mahan, the rather frail son of an Irish immigrant carpenter, was determined to excel as a cadet at West Point despite his physical limitations. Superintendent Thayer had just instituted his practice of having the cadet companies divided into sections of twelve to fifteen people for class study when Mahan was a plebe, and because there was not enough faculty to teach such small groups, Thayer appointed cadets to teach some sections. Mahan for the last three years he spent as a cadet was both first in his class and an instructor in mathematics. As soon as he graduated, he was detailed as assistant professor of mathematics and principal assistant professor of engineering. After two years of teaching, he applied for a leave of absence to go to Europe. With Thayer's encouragement, Mahan took a four year course at the French School for Engineers and Artillerists at Metz, doing special research into the latest advances in European civil engineering in roads, railroads, and waterways.

Mahan was an engineering genius who had the ability to synthesize what he observed and write about it theoretically. He rarely left West Point after his return from France, and in fact it was said of him that "he never saw battle—and never went for a walk without an umbrella." Through his teaching and writing, however, he influenced the campaigns

The ramparts at the edge of the bluff overlooking the Hudson made a popular promenade for visitors to West Point during the 19th century.

of the entire Civil War. Fifty-five out of the sixty most important battles were commanded by West Point graduates, Northern and Southern, who had taken Mahan's courses and read his book: *Advanced Guard, Outpost, and Detachment Service of Troops, with the Essential Principles of Strategy and Grand Tactics*, known familiarly as "Outpost."

Mahan's theories of strategy emphasized speed and maneuverability rather than total destruction of the enemy forces. He taught that according to the lessons of history, particularly the campaigns of Frederick the Great and Napoleon (whom Mahan revered), capturing key cities and posts of the enemy and then striking the opposing forces with maximum maneuverability were most likely to lead to victory. One ironic reason for the duration and extreme devastation of the Civil War was the skill exhibited by the generals of both sides who had been taught by Mahan. He himself was particularly outraged by the printing of pirated editions of "Outpost" in the South during the War.

Mahan only spent a little of his course time on "The Art of War," however, although that was the most popular part of it, and much more on civil engineering. Through the 1830s and into the 1840s it was the engineering reputation that was going to save West Point from hostile popular sentiment and consolidate its reputation. When cadets graduated and were given a temporary rank known as a brevet rank, they had only a limited obligation for Army service. In a nation where "soldiering" was not particularly respected and where the only active military life was on the frontier, many did indeed leave the Army. Their employment as engineers in a country where no such profession had existed until the military academy began its course of study was assured—and so were their contributions to the nation's welfare. The Committee on Military Affairs, reporting to the House of Representatives on March 17, 1834, noted:

The railroads which connect the capital of Massachusetts with the 'heart' of the state and with important harbors in Rhode Island and Connecticut ... the Susquehanna & Baltimore and Baltimore and Ohio Railroads; ... the new roads which have augmented the wealth of the Territories of

Michigan and Arkansas ... important harbor improvements upon the shores of the lakes and upon the seacoast are some of the enduring memorials of the usefulness of the Military Academy....

The engineers who did not pursue active careers often helped to establish schools of engineering or programs based on West Point's. Harvard offered an engineering curriculum in 1847 with West Point graduates for faculty; Yale did the same in 1852. Of the eight civilian technological colleges in the country in 1860, seven used the West Point curriculum and had West Point graduates on their staffs.

The names of the engineers, both Army men and those who had resigned to work as civilians, read like a roster of the great names of 19th century America. The natural dredging process built into the Mississippi River, which saved St. Louis as a port, was accomplished by 2nd Lt. Robert E. Lee, Class of 1829, and the leader of a reconnaissance party to find the best route for the transcontinental railroad was George B. McClellan, Class of 1846, who would be the commander-in-chief of the Union forces for the first part of the Civil War. The inventor of the locomotive whistle that screamed out across the nation for more than one hundred years as a symbol of mobility and communication was railroad engineer George Washington Whistler, Class of 1819, father of James Abbott McNeill Whistler, artist and drop-out of the Class of 1854.

The consistent cry of the Jacksonian objectors to West Point was that it was a place of privilege, breeding a useless military aristocracy. These objections were fueled periodically by tracts such as "Military Academy Unmasked, or Corruption and Military Despotism Exposed," written in 1830 by the embittered Captain Alden Partridge. As the 1830s waned in a national economic depression, the popularity of the Jacksonians themselves grew less, however. And as the network of roads, railroads, and canals that West Point-trained engineers had built spread systematically across the country, the value of the Academy was acknowledged. In the 1840s there were still grumblers, but the 1840s brought a war, and the Academy, which had been going through its growing pains, met the challenge with dispatch and glory.

Cadets lounge under the trees along a dirt road in the mid-19th century when West Point presented a leisurely, bucolic image.

THE PROVING YEARS

One of the first to describe West Point in the 1840s was Charles Dickens, who visited the United States in 1841 and wrote up his reactions in his generally irascible *American Notes*. He paints a very sympathetic picture of the Academy, and this, coming from such a biased source, has unusual credibility.

> *... along a glittering path of sunlit water with here and there a skiff, whose white sail often bends on some new track as sudden flaws of wind come down upon her from the gullies in the hills: hemmed in, besides, all round with memories of Washington, and events of the revolutionary war: is the Military School of America.*

> *It could not stand on more appropriate ground, and any ground more beautiful can hardly be. The course of education is severe, but well devised and manly. . . .*

> *The beauty and freshness of this calm retreat, in the very dawn and greenness of summer—it was then the beginning of June— were exquisite indeed.*

West Point's increasing security in the success of its own functions and place in the world seems reflected in Dickens's serene landscape. The faculty were innovative and energetic for those days, and its influence was felt throughout the country. The cadets were, for the most part, eager to be there.

Foreign military expert Thaddeus Kosciusko, while in charge of West Point's defenses in 1778 during the Revolutionary War, designed this rock garden for his own amusement.

The South Boat Landing (left) was long the only real access to the Academy. When Congress authorized a road north in 1863, the Superintendent said, "It would be ruinous to the morals and discipline of the Corps."

Molding A Cadet

Cadet life as it had evolved from the rag-tag early days through the times of boyish rebellion against Partridge's martinet attitude had come into a golden age. Under Superintendent Thayer the minute time schedule that accounted for each particle of the day and the rigid discipline that Partridge had drawn up had been effectively enforced. Thayer's system of demerits, which counted in the weekly ranking along with academic points, assured constant attention to detail and constant vigilance. However, Thayer had also been firm on two points about attitude. One was that there was to be absolutely no favoritism, and the scheme of daily class recitations and demerits for faulty behavior encouraged that; the complementary attitude was that if every cadet was equal, each was also equally a gentleman. Hazing new cadets, which assumed destructive proportions later in the Academy's life, was therefore limited to the first month of a plebe's summer camp and consisted of rather innocent high jinks. Cadet Morris Schaff described his hazing in the summer of 1858 as "irritating and sometimes funny" and noted that it died away after the first month. Hazing in those days was characterized by such wit as cutting the ropes on a tent where plebes were sleeping so they were suddenly smothered by a deluge of canvas, or stealing their clothes so they had to report for morning drill wrapped in blankets. When they visited in later years, veterans of pre-Civil War West Point were shocked at the brutal extremes to which hazing had developed and at the fact that it was condoned.

The lack of favoritism inherent in the system of making each man perform every day was not only character building, but also necessary by the 1840s. With West Point's increasing success, it became prestigious to be a graduate, and many prominent families were eager to secure appointments for their sons. Two generations of Duponts, already successful proprietors of a munitions business and socially prominent, attended West Point before the Civil War, as well as the grandsons of Alexander Hamilton and President Martin Van Buren. In the 1850s there was a Washington from Virginia, a Buchanan from Pennsylvania, and a Vanderbilt from New York. Of course, there were also the sons of prominent military men. Although many of these cadets' families were very vocal about not wanting special privileges for their offspring, they often meant the reverse. In any other atmosphere money and privilege would have told far more than they did at West Point.

Charles Dickens noted: "The number of cadets being about equal to that of the members of Congress, one is sent here from every Congressional District: its member influencing the selection." In fact it was not quite that simple, and it was not regularized by an act of Congress until 1843. Before then it had been the practice for the Secretary of War to appoint officially one cadet from each Congressional district on the recommendation of the congressman from that district. This was legally recognized in 1843, along with power granted to the President to appoint ten "at-large" cadets, who were usually the sons of career officers. These young men had rarely lived in one location long enough for their families to secure a Congressional appointment. The number of cadets had been raised to 250 by Superintendent Swift and only very very slowly did it grow to double that during the rest of the 19th century. Although there were allegations of political favoritism in the appointment of cadets and although favoritism certainly did occur, there were also cadets like farmer's son Morris Schaff, tanner's son Ulysses S. Grant, and Thomas J. Jackson (later immortalized as "Stonewall"), who came in from the hills of western Virginia, where he had been a local constable.

The academic entrance requirements were deliberately kept to the minimum so there would be equality of opportunity for those whose families were well off enough to have paid for good educations and for those who could get only to backwoods schools. As a result of the low entrance requirements there was a high rate of dropping out by those who could not meet the strain of the course work (Dickens was told that ". . .not more than half the number who begin their studies here ever remain to finish them."), and the entrance requirements were a bone of contention between the superintendent and the faculty on the one hand and Congress and the War Department on the other. Nevertheless, they remained low.

The entrance examinations were the new cadets' first encounter with the military manner. The

examinations consisted of doing simple arithmetic problems and problems in fractions, reading from an assigned selection, and writing some dictated sentences, but they were conducted in front of the Academic Board. The superintendent, the commandant, and the faculty who sat on the board seemed to Morris Schaff "a formidable reality to youthful eyes." To Edward Hartz a few years earlier they seemed "the most rigid, cold and merciless looking set of men I ever before beheld. They seemed so much oppressed by the weight of dignity that rests upon them, that a kind look was as much a stranger to their faces, as good living has been to me since I have landed here."

For those cadets who survived the examination, scholastically and psychologically (usually about two thirds to three fourths of those who took it),

Between the Mexican War and the Civil War the photographed serenity and formality of West Point life belied the energy of the Academy. On Sunday afternoons, one of their few free periods, cadets gathered in such places as this promontory with its river view.

the next step was being fitted for a uniform and buying needed supplies at the commissaries. One of Thayer's gestures toward creating equality among the cadets was to limit their pay to $28 a month and refuse them permission to receive any additional funds from home. The $28 they never saw; it was redeemable at the commissary in razors, clothes, and books. The allowance was rarely high enough to meet daily demands, so most cadets were in debt for necessities most of the time.

The cadets were reduced to desperate extremes at times in their attempts to raise spending money. Although both alcohol and tobacco were forbidden, their use was not unknown (one cadet said he had never seen so much tobacco smoked in his life), and cadets were ingenious in getting them without any money at all. Morris Schaff and a friend traded their civilian clothes for some "poor whiskey and some kind of berry pie" to a fellow across the river.

Failed Cadets: Poe and Whistler

Although the records of West Point's graduates impressed the nation, there were also cadets who failed to graduate while leaving a mark at the Academy and becoming widely acclaimed in other fields. Well before the Civil War the presence of Edgar Allan Poe and James McNeill Whistler carried eventual reverberations that were combined of equal parts of their unsuitability as cadets and their later fame.

Poe, who entered West Point on July 1, 1830, after serving two years in the Army, came to the Academy purely as a means of getting an education and reconciling himself with his adopted father. He had already published two volumes of poetry, but, at the age of twenty-one, he had no means of supporting himself apart from the military. When his adopted father married for a second time in October 1830 and disowned him, Poe did everything he could to get himself dismissed, including spending time

Edgar Allan Poe, who dropped out of the Class of 1834, was miserable during his time at West Point, despite encouragement from Colonel Thayer in publishing a volume of poetry.

at the tavern of Benny Havens (whom he called "the only congenial soul in this god-forsaken place") and ignoring roll call. Before he was dismissed in March 1831, he had succeeded in making the acquaintance of Superintendent Thayer, who was always a man to recognize talent, however unsuitable it might have been for the Academy, and who even helped Poe publish yet another volume of poetry. Poe had showed some of his work to Thayer, who commended his desire to publish. Poe pointed out, however, that he would need money to advance a publisher, so Thayer recommended that Poe get subscriptions from his fellow cadets by implying that the poems made fun of the staff. Poe collected the money and dedicated the book to the cadets. Their reactions to the published poems have not been recorded.

James Abbott McNeill Whistler, a non-graduate of the Class of 1855, drew in "Asleep on the Post" a lackadaisical sentry who may have reflected his own attitude toward the Academy's attempts to instill spit and polish among the cadets.

Second half hour

Whistler's sketches of West Point life good-humoredly focused on cadet lapses, such as a sentry who becomes progressively less attentive during a tour of guard duty.

On Post in Camp.

Last Half Hour!

Cadets traditionally took visiting ladies for a stroll along Flirtation Walk, a sylvan pathway that remained popular even in the late 20th century.

When James Abbott McNeill Whistler arrived at the Academy in 1851, he was barely seventeen and the scion of a military family. His grandfather had fought for the British in the Revolution, then returned to America after the conclusion of the war and enlisted in the American army; his father, George Washington Whistler, Class of 1819, had graduated from West Point and later resigned from the Army to pursue a distinguished career as a civil engineer. The senior Whistler's death in St. Petersburg, Russia, in 1849, while building the Moscow-St. Petersburg railroad, determined Mrs. Whistler, whose brother was a distinguished graduate of the Class of 1817, to enlist "Jimmie" in the military academy. (George Washington Whistler's career is one of the surest and most dazzling proofs of the preeminence of West Point as an engineering school in the first half of the 19th century.) James Whistler was completely unfitted for life at the Academy, but his personality was so ebullient that he seemed to ride the crest of the waves of discipline, rather than being drowned by them as Poe had been.

There are many famous stories about Whistler's cockiness in the face of military demand, but two represent his strength of character and certainty of talent, on the one hand, and how unfitted he was for the Academy on the other. Whistler was usually first in Professor Robert Weir's drawing class despite his great fear of being corrected, but supposedly in one exercise he drew a bridge as assigned and then for artistic embellishment drew three boys lounging on it. Reprimanded for having placed the boys in what was essentially an engineering exercise, Whistler made the drawing again, this time putting the boys on the river bank below the bridge. Reprimanded a second time, Whistler drew the bridge once more and this time removed all human life from the scene, merely placing little grave stones on the bank.

Whistler's dismissal from West Point after three years of mutual aggravation was precipitated in science class. (Poe had written a sonnet at West Point twenty years before called "Science" in which he asked, "Why preyest thou thus upon the poet's heart,/Vulture, whose wings are dull realities?") When Whistler was asked in the daily recitation to describe the properties of silicon, he began, "Silicon is a gas . . . ." Told to stop at that point, he later would say, "Had silicon been a gas, I would have been a major general."

Summer Camp

Summer camp, into which the plebes entered, somewhat mitigated the austerity forecast by the Academic Board at the examination. It was one of the pleasanter institutions of 19th century West Point life. From early June through August, the entire Corps of Cadets, except for those on furlough between their second and third years, encamped on "the Plain"—the level plateau above the Hudson that the Academy buildings surrounded. The Camp was set up as soon as the June graduation ceremonies were over. One cadet from the 1850s remembered: "When the graduating exercises were over, the battalion formed in front of the barracks, and, with the band at its head, the colors proudly borne, marched across the Plain to the camping ground. . . . I remember very well the pleasing activity as soon as ranks were broken and my surprise at seeing the tents go up so quickly, converting the site, like magic, into a little white city."

Uniforms, discipline, and weaponry changed little at West Point from the mid-19th century, when it was an innovative institution, to the early 20th century, when it was static. This artillery exercise near the end of the century could have been the same fifty years earlier.

43

Although cadets unbent during summer camp when there were frequent "hops" or dances for visiting ladies, it is doubtful if any sentry ever actually waltzed away from his sentry box.

It was at summer camp, whose administration was relegated almost completely to the commandant and the tactical department, that the cadets learned about practical soldiering. The junior classes learned infantry tactics and spent hours on end drilling. The Department of War would use the Corps of Cadets to test the speed and maneuverability of new drills developed in response to new weapons. There were regular visits by committees from Washington—as well as tourists from New York and Saratoga Springs and the hotels along the Hudson—who came to see the spruce young West Pointers forward march and turn on a dime, making perfect corners. The four company commanders were extremely competitive among themselves, each striving to have his own company drill the most efficiently. First Class cadets who would graduate the next year were taught during summer camp to manufacture ammunition and learned advanced artillery procedures. In the same way that the War Department experimented with drilling with the junior classes, they used the First Classmen to experiment with advanced pieces of new artillery. One memorable piece of gunnery was the gigantic Columbiad, which was designed to be used on the seacoast for defense against enemy shipping.

Life in summer camp for the cadets was softened by the weather and the holiday conditions of living out of doors. Although the training was rigorous, as it always was at West Point, it bore almost no resemblance to the filth and hazards of real war. Even the most complicated tasks, such as building a pontoon bridge, tended to end in a frolic. It was during the summer that cadets had their few glimpses of young ladies, who could not be expected to visit during the winter when there was the chance of their being marooned overnight by a freeze on the river. One of the required activities for cadets was dancing, which was classed with fencing as an accomplishment suitable for a gentleman. In the winter in the fencing academy the cadets solemnly waltzed, polkaed, and square-danced with each other under the eye of the Italian dancing master who during the Civil War would be promoted to commander of a black regiment. But in the summer there were "hops"—as 19th century dances were called—where girls in hoop skirts, properly chaperoned, whirled around the floor with cadets, perhaps after taking an afternoon stroll down "Flirtation Walk," a heavily wooded path that wound toward the river.

The Mexican War

Finally, in 1846 the results of long halcyon summers with their tactical training and the carefully accumulated engineering skills built up in the curriculum over the decades were tested. On Monday, May 11, 1846, in response to a cavalry skirmish between Mexican troops and United States dragoons on the disputed Texas-Mexico border, President James K. Polk declared in a message to Congress: "The cup of forbearance has been exhausted. After reiterated menaces, Mexico has passed the boundary of the United States, has invaded our territory and shed American blood upon the American soil." At West Point the response to this war—now often perceived to have been provoked by the United States as a way of annexing Texas and California—was simple jubilation: "War at last sure enough! Ain't it glorious!" exulted a cadet.

One reason for the cadet's excitement was that a war meant that graduates would have a chance to prove themselves and to launch real careers in the Army, rather than languishing in coastal forts where they would have to serve as quartermasters, or enduring the fearful isolation of frontier posts.

Even though West Point's prestige and perceived value had increased enormously, there still were occasional mutterings that sifted through from Congress about the school breeding a useless military elite. The prestige of the military itself was not high. Ulysses S. Grant, Class of 1843, tells of riding proudly through the streets of Cincinnati wearing his uniform soon after graduation. He assumed that everyone was looking at him with awe when "a little urchin, bareheaded, barefooted, with dirty and ragged pants held up by a single gallows . . . turned

One of the earliest surviving photographs of a West Point graduate is this Daguerreotype of Ulysses S. Grant, Class of 1843, taken in Louisiana in 1845. Grant came to dislike wearing uniforms early in his career.

to me and cried: 'Soldier! will you work? No sirree; I'll sell my shirt first!!'" Grant claimed never to have recovered from the "distaste for the military uniform" that this incident gave him. Perhaps the earliest photograph in this book is the misty Daguerreotype from this period, which shows an unrecognizable young Grant in a splendid military cap and tight jacket, frowning into the camera when he was on duty in New Orleans. The slight foppishness of the uniform suggests how incongruous it must have appeared in rough frontier towns.

The Mexican War would change all that, however. Although Americans never took much to uniforms as such, the connotations of the uniform and West Point were changed forever. The war was a valuable proving ground. Almost all of the Civil War commanders served in it, and of the 523 West Point graduates who served, 452 received honorary promotions. The importance of the Mexican War for West Point's reputation cannot be exaggerated. It finally firmly established the value of the Academy. Lt. Gen. Winfield Scott, Commander in Chief of the United States Army—and not a West Pointer himself—wrote in 1860 that:

I give it as my fixed opinion, that but for our graduated cadets, the war between the United States and Mexico might, and probably would, have lasted some four or five years, with, in its first half, more defeats than victories falling to our share; whereas in less than two campaigns, we conquered a great country and a peace, without the loss of a single battle or skirmish.

The Impact of Delafield and Lee

During the years between 1840 and the Civil War, West Point was governed by only three superintendents. Richard Delafield was superintendent for two different periods (1838–1845 and 1856–1861), and Robert E. Lee was an immensely popular superintendent from 1852 until 1855. The unpopular Henry Brewerton was superintendent from 1845 until 1852. Delafield and Lee left their marks, however, in very different ways.

Described by a plebe at the entrance examination as "a pudgy man with heavy, sandy eyebrows, abundant grayish sandy hair and a

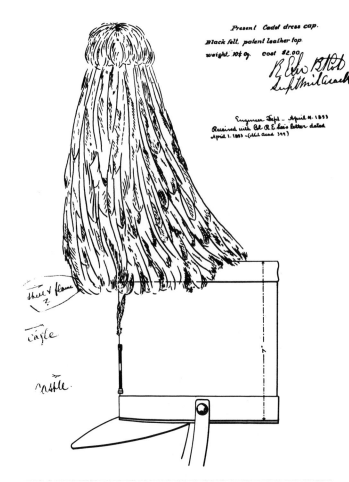

The modified cap (above) designed by Col. Robert E. Lee, superintendent of the Academy, in 1853, replaced an original version that weighed five pounds. Superintendent Lee's cap weighed a mere 10¼ ounces, a reduction welcomed by cadets.

General Winfield Scott (right), although not a West Point graduate, became a staunch friend of the Academy and attributed the Mexican War successes to the officers trained at West Point. The cadet uniform was modeled on those worn by Scott's troops in the War of 1812.

47

pronounced eagle nose," Delafield was a man of detail, concerned about practical matters of administration, and inclined to be fussy. He—with the other superintendents of this period—fought to keep the superintendency of West Point under the Corps of Engineers rather than having superintendents appointed at the discretion of the War Department from all branches of the Army, and he improved communication and relations between the Academy and Congress. Delafield also was responsible for the martial English Tudor architecture that characterizes the look of West Point to this day. The first architecturally significant building at West Point had been the Old Chapel, built in 1836 just before Delafield's tenure, in the fashionable Classical Revival style. This building, now located at the entrance to the cemetery, set the custom of using locally quarried granite. When Delafield came, newly fashionable Gothic and Romanesque Revival styles of architecture were being seen in the cities,

Superintendent Thomas G. Pitcher, Class of 1845, sits with his wife on the porch of the superintendent's quarters (above) *built by Sylvanus Thayer.*

Cadets lined up outside the Old Barracks (right) *presented a halcyon scene to summer visitors, who had only a dim notion of the rigors of winter training.*

and he adopted the English Tudor variation of this as more appropriate to a military atmosphere. Crenelated towers, heavy arches, and slit windows, all in the overwhelmingly austere gray stone, were Delafield's delight. While he was at West Point the library, the riding hall, new stables, a new mess hall, and a new barracks were all erected.

Lee did as much for the Academy's already lustrous image during his tenure as Delafield did for its appearance. Lee had graduated second in his class at West Point and served brilliantly in the Corps of Engineers and the Mexican War. He was the perfect gentleman without being in any way weak or humorless and was a universal favorite. When he reprimanded a cadet who had been fighting with another by saying, "Don't you think that it is better for brothers to dwell together in peace and harmony?", the cadet replied, "Yes, Colonel, and if we were all like you, it would be an easy thing to do." In the higher reaches of the military and the government, Lee enjoyed an equally favorable reputation. General Scott thought that Lee was certain to be general in chief of the Army someday.

It was under Lee's superintendency that the first major change was made in the curriculum since Thayer's time. Despite West Point's solid prestige,

Robert E. Lee (above) *was one of the Academy's most popular superintendents, serving 1852–1855.*

With the Hudson River close at hand, bridge-building training, like this pontoon bridge exercise, could always be done "in the field."

accusations had been made that the academy concentrated too much on engineering, to the detriment of practical field training and such liberal arts courses appropriate to gentlemen and officers as literature and languages. French, for instance, while a requirement, was only taught as a language to be read. One Mexican War veteran said, "I have since learned more Spanish from Mexican senoritas in two months than I did French at the Point in two years." In 1854, Lee proposed to remedy this by extending the course from four years to five years. He began by dividing the plebes into two classes, with the younger ones commencing a five year program. There was opposition to this from Congress, and in 1858 the course was switched back. The West Point faculty liked it, however, so it was switched back again and in 1860 a Congressional commission was appointed to investigate the merits of the two plans.

The Davis Commission

The commission was named after its head, Senator Jefferson Davis, a former Secretary of War, who made the trip to West Point with his fellow commissioners several times during the summer and autumn of 1860. The other members of the commission included another senator, two members of the House, and two Army officers. Morris Schaff remembered Davis, a member of the Class of 1828, "walking . . . under the elms mottling green and gold, in the autumn of 1860 . . . I recall him arrayed in a dark blue flannel suit, I can see his square shoulders, military walk and lithe figure. Had I known then, as I passed him from time to time in company with professors who had been his fellow cadets, what I know now, I should certainly have gazed wonderingly into his spare, resolute, and rather pleading face . . . ."

Another visitor that autumn was the Prince of Wales, Queen Victoria's son, who would not become King Edward VII for another forty years. The Prince's visit seemed nearly incredible at the time. It was the first time a member of the English royal family had ever visited America, in colonial days or after independence. The sign of West Point's importance was the Prince's voyage upriver in the revenue cutter "Harriet Lane," named after President James Buchanan's niece and hostess. Schaff wrote:

A view taken from Garrison Ferry, the connection between the railroad on the Hudson's east bank and West Point, is one of the earliest photographs of the Academy.

The royal party arrived at the wharf about 3 PM and was met by the adjutant. Mounted on horses especially provided for the occasion, the Prince and his party were escorted to Colonel Delafield's quarters by the detachment of regular dragoons on duty at the Post. On reaching the Plain a national salute was fired from Battery Knox, the hills echoing grandly with each discharge.

Less than a year later the hills of Virginia would echo with the discharges of the first battles of the Civil War. It would then be known that the truly remarkable visit was not that of the Prince of Wales but that of Jefferson Davis. Sophisticated Southerners such as Davis and Lee had hoped to avoid war until it actually occurred. Up until the last minute they performed their duties for the United States as conscientiously as possible. Lee was even offered command of the Northern forces. Just

In 1860 cadets posed in front of the Academic Building on one of the Academy's fire engines. The symmetry and composition suggest how the technical limitations and aesthetics of 19th century photography complemented the formality of Academy life.

as a piece of dry wood may flare up and burn more brilliantly just before exploding into a shower of sparks, so the constellation of Southern administrators and visitors under the analytical Davis Commission shed light on every aspect of the military academy, just before the Commission, half of the Academy student body, and the nation itself exploded into the conflagration of the war. Historian Stephen Ambrose points out that "unlike the Jacksonians, most of the critics of West Point of the forties and fifties were friendly; in fact, most were graduates. The Academy was an institution to which most Americans looked with pride." The Davis Commission neatly summarized the civilian and military accomplishments of West Pointers,

detailing the vast public works and engineering achievements as well as their crucial wartime contributions. The commission's report also called for the reorganization of the Academy, but there was no time to act upon it.

On April 12, 1861, within months of the publishing of the Davis Commission report, General P.G.T. Beauregard, West Point graduate and briefly its superintendent, opened fire on Fort Sumter in the harbor of Charleston, South Carolina. The war had begun, and the "best qualities of the soldiers" the Davis Commission found at West Point would be put to the severest test.

Jefferson Davis, Class of 1828, U.S. Secretary of War, and President of the Confederate States of America, coordinated the Davis Commission Report in 1860.

At Antietam, on October 3, 1862, President Abraham Lincoln (right), *towering over the officers of the Army of the Potomac in his stovepipe hat, visited Gen. George B. McClellan, Class of 1846.*

THE CIVIL WAR AND FRONTIER CAMPAIGNS

The last of early West Point's tests in the popular mind came in January 1863, at the nadir of the Civil War for the North. Following almost two years of defeats and difficult campaigns in the war, the annual bill for funding for the Academy came up to the Senate. So unhappy was the government with the way the war was going and so determined were the Radical Republicans in government to blame it on the generals who had a West Point education—

with all the old criticisms of elitism and of theoretical rather than practical training—that the motion was made to abolish the Academy altogether. Senator James Lane of Kansas suggested that if the Union were defeated—which seemed all too likely at that point—the epitaph should be: "Died of West Point pro-slaveryism." The most disturbing concomitants to the Northern defeats under West Point-trained Generals George B. McClellan, Henry

Lt. Gen. Thomas "Stonewall" Jackson, Class of 1846, conducted lightning raids against Union forces until his death at Chancellorsville in 1863.

Gen. Robert E. Lee, Class of 1829, poses with his son (left), Maj. Gen. George Washington Custis Lee, Class of 1854, near the end of the Civil War. Robert embodied the qualities of gentlemanliness, strength, and decisiveness that West Point sought to inculcate in its graduates.

Halleck, and Ambrose Burnside were the Southern victories under West Point-trained Generals Lee, Stonewall Jackson, and Joseph Johnston. The only conclusion that the Northern Radicals could draw was that West Point, if not a school that produced incompetents, was a breeding ground for traitors.

The movement to abolish the Academy was defeated, but by a majority of only 29 to 10, which shows that at least one quarter of the United States senators then in office thought that their constituents would not object to the elimination of the military academy. By July 1863, with the victories at Gettysburg and Vicksburg turning the tide, Ulysses S. Grant, William Tecumseh Sherman, George Meade, and Philip Sheridan were becoming heroes. West Point's honor, for the North at least, was saved.

Perhaps ironically, the entire dilemma originated with the fact that West Point contributed so

Gen. Joe Johnston, Class of 1829, was a good tactician and a bulwark of the Confederate Army, but he failed to attack and press an advantage when he had one, and he remained at odds with President Jefferson Davis.

Ulysses S. Grant, the greatest Union commander, was described by West Point Professor Dennis Mahan as "a mental machine ... of the powerful low-pressure class, which ... drives all obstacles before it."

many leaders to both the Union and the Confederate forces. Of the sixty major battles of the war, fifty-five of them were commanded *on both sides* by West Point graduates, and the other five battles had a West Point-trained commander on at least one side. The very first action of the war, the firing on Fort Sumter by Confederate troops on April 12, 1861, proves the point. The troops were commanded to fire by General P.G.T. Beauregard, Class of 1838, who only two and a half months before had briefly been superintendent of the Academy. (Beauregard was appointed to succeed Delafield and is reported to have told a cadet from his home state of Louisiana who asked him whether he, the cadet, should resign to go South or not, "Watch me; and when I jump, you jump. What's the use of jumping too soon?" After five days as superintendent, Beauregard learned that Louisiana had left the Union and he "jumped.") The lanyard of the guns firing on Fort Sumter was pulled by Wade Hampton Gibbes, who had graduated less than a year before from the Academy; and the Union commander of Fort Sumter was Major Robert Anderson, Class of 1826, who had been Beauregard's artillery instructor at West Point.

The Atmosphere at West Point

The actual beginning of the war released sectional tension that had built up over the preceding decade at West Point more intensely than in the rest of the country. In 1861 there were two West Point graduating classes because of the innovation of the five-year program that Robert E. Lee had initiated when he was superintendent. From these classes a total of forty-five young officers would fight on both sides at the first Battle of Bull Run in July 1861.

Maj. Gen. William Tecumseh Sherman, Class of 1840, pauses near Atlanta in 1864 as the grim embodiment of his dictum: "War is hell." He later advocated a postwar policy of moderation toward the Indians.

Until April, when the war had begun, the attention at West Point had been concentrated for the most part on the Southerners who advocated secession and rebellion. The Southerners were rabid about their allegiances. There were a number of fights and at least one duel; after the raid at Harper's Ferry, John Brown's body was hanged in effigy from a barracks window. When cadets resigned to "go South," it was a romantic act and there was a certain glamor to it. The trend started with red-haired, high-tempered Henry S. Farley of South Carolina, who left on November 19, 1860, one day and one month before South Carolina seceded. An Alabama cadet who left in December 1860 called the cadets to attention in the Mess Hall and spoke to them, concluding, "Battalion, attention! Good-bye, boys! God bless you all!" after which the cadets lifted him to their shoulders and carried him down to the wharf. Morris Schaff remembered that after the speeches and traditional celebration on Washington's Birthday, February 22, 1861, when the band came through the sally port into the central quadrangle of the barracks playing the "Star-Spangled Banner," Schaff and Custer led a cheer from their lighted window. Custer's roommate, Thomas Lafayette Rosser, led a chorus of "Dixie" from another window. The cheers and singing echoed back and forth from different sides of the barracks. Rosser would fight Custer up and down the Shenandoah Valley in 1864 and then, a decade later, defeated and working as chief engineer for the Northern Pacific Railroad, renewed his friendship with Custer, whose cavalrymen protected the railroad's surveyors.

The strong bonds of camaraderie forged at West Point survived the sectional competition there and, as the story of Custer and Rosser suggests, usually survived the real horrors of the war. U.S. Grant (Class of 1843) sent congratulations across the trenches at Petersburg, Virginia, to George Pickett (Class of 1846) on the birth of Pickett's child. John Lea, Confederate States of America (CSA) and Class of 1861, was married while a prisoner of war and his best man was his classmate and Union officer George Armstrong Custer; General Dodson Ramseur, CSA, died in the arms of Academy classmates at General Philip Sheridan's Union headquarters.

These gestures from a more courtly and florid age than our own are not necessarily mere romance.

Epitomizing the personal bonds between West Pointers, George Armstrong Custer poses solemnly with James B. Washington, a captured Confederate officer who had resigned from the Academy and the Class of 1863 when war threatened in 1861.

The Academy was one of the strongest defining experiences in any young man's life and because of its genuinely national character it operated as one of the few consistently unifying agencies in the young and divisive United States. Thus, the apprehension felt by Congress in 1863 was partly a feeling that a West Point allegiance might transcend a division of loyalties. If the South was winning, perhaps Northern generals wanted it that way. This, of course, was not true, but one of the reasons the Civil War was particularly bloody was the very expertise instilled in its generals on both sides by West Point.

The Battle of Gettysburg

Gettysburg, with Vicksburg one of the two most significant battles of the war, is a case in point. Until the Battle of Gettysburg there were several broad reasons for the South's winning the war; such Southern generals as Joe Johnston and Stonewall Jackson had never left the military from the time of their graduation from West Point until the war began, whereas the Northern generals such as Grant, Sherman, and McClellan had diverged into civilian pursuits in the years before the war, and it took them some time to reacclimate themselves. The Southern generals also were leading an army of enthusiasts, who were, for the most part, outdoorsmen acquainted with guns and horses in private life and who were fighting a war that was psychologically on the offensive—the South wanted independence. Territorially the Southern armies were fighting defensively on home ground with a friendly civilian population. In addition, the North had difficulty finding a commanding general who had the ability of Lee.

A Union staff conference brought together several West Pointers who made their mark during the Civil War and earned more laurels afterward (from left): Wesley Merritt, Philip Sheridan, George Crook, James Forsyth, and George Custer.

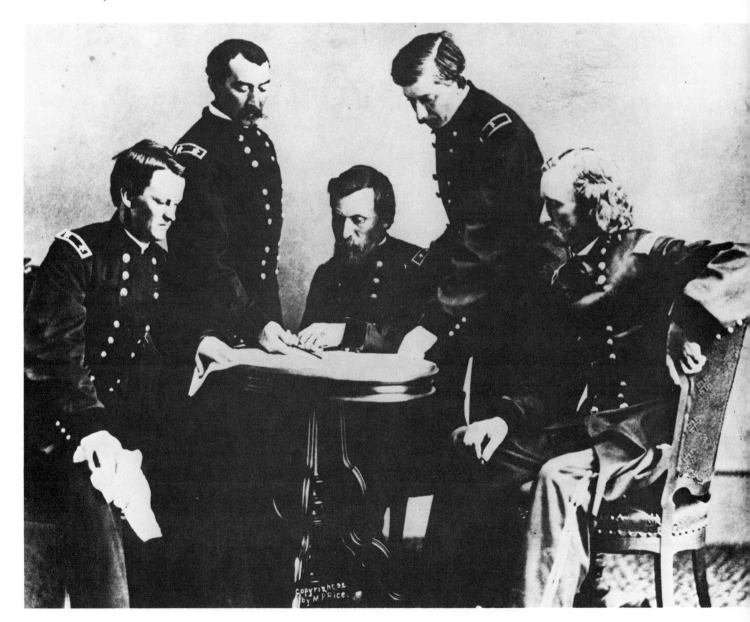

By 1863, however, the fighting skills on both sides had been honed sharp. That year Lee decided that an invasion of the North might decimate Northern morale as well as territory and that an invasion would enhance the South's position in its negotiations with England. In addition, the South might have the chance to sue for peace if it won on Northern soil. Lee marched the Army of Northern Virginia, 76,000 strong, into Pennsylvania on June 27. General George Meade (Class of 1835) commanded the Northern Army of the Potomac, which followed Lee into Pennsylvania from where they had been fighting (and losing) in Virginia. Lee committed one error that, although serious in any army before the airplane made reconnaissance easy, was particularly deadly in the Civil War. He let Jeb Stuart, his cavalry commander, go off on a raid of his own and thereby lost the "eyes and ears" of his army. Then, in a second error, against which Professor Mahan warned in the familiar West Point text known as "Outpost," Lee abandoned his defensive position on the side of South Mountain, near Gettysburg, to do battle with Meade. The terrain, therefore, with its lethal valley between two ridges, had been chosen by neither general. The importance of terrain was emphasized on the second day of the battle, July 2,

J.E.B. Stuart, Class of 1854, one of the most audacious Confederate cavalry leaders, commanded the Army of Northern Virginia's cavalry at his death in 1864.

when Gouvernor Kemble Warren, Chief Engineer of the Army of the Potomac, climbed up on Little Round Top Hill to find that he could see the countryside for miles around, including the lines of the Confederates across the valley on Seminary Ridge and the Union lines to the North. Realizing that possession of Little Round Top gave a vantage over the entire valley, including both Union and Confederate lines, Warren simultaneously sent to General Meade to urge that the hill be occupied and commandeered the first troops he could find in Meade's name to do so. The next day the Confederates attacked across the open valley in the charge directed

Taken just after the Battle of Gettysburg, Alexander Gardner's "Rebel Sharpshooter at Devil's Den" captured the drama of war instead of the personal qualities of a formal portrait.

Typical of the small towns that the war decimated was Harper's Ferry (above), Virginia (now West Virginia), where John Brown staged his raid in 1859.

The tardy supply wagons (right) of Maj. Gen. George Meade were here photographed after the Battle of Gettysburg, waiting to cross the flooded Potomac over which Robert E. Lee and his forces had already escaped.

by George E. Pickett, the last graduate in the Class of 1846, and were defeated, but had they been able to get Little Round Top, they could have enfiladed the entire Union position.

When combat was over on July 3, the Confederates, who had failed to take the Union line, limped back to their own lines. Lee remained defiantly in position over July 4, but neither then nor on July 5, when he had retreated as far into Maryland as the flooded Potomac would allow, did Meade follow the Confederates. Professor Mahan had once written, "A battle gained is always a fine thing; but . . . [if we] simply force him to retreat without further loss

than that on the battlefield . . . the enemy will soon be able to rally his forces and offer a new battle." Lee knew this and had expected pursuit from Meade who *should* have known it. Later in the war Lee guarded against pursuit when he fought Grant, whose great strength, Lee well understood, was that he *would* pursue doggedly and as long as his men could walk.

In the Battle of Gettysburg those classes of young officers who graduated in May and June 1861 suffered particularly. Lt. Malbone·Watson, May Class of 1861, received a serious leg wound on Little Round Top and returned, one-legged, to West Point to teach French for the duration of the war. Charles Edward Hazlett, also in the May Class of 1861, bent down to listen to the final orders of dying Brigadier General Stephen Weed, who was lying beside the gun that Watson had been operating, when he caught a bullet and fell dead over Weed's still breathing body. George Augustus Woodruff, from the June 1861 class, was wounded just before Pickett's famous charge, known as the "High Water Mark of the Confederacy," and his June classmate Alonzo Cushing was wounded twice but continued to whisper orders and fired his last gun just as he got a bullet in his brain.

General Grant and his staff gather in camp at City Point, Virginia, in June 1864, a time when the North was pushing hard against a weakening Confederacy.

The Vicksburg Campaign

Vicksburg, the other turning-point battle of the Civil War, illustrated just as much as Gettysburg the tactical brilliance that was West Point's heritage and the suffering that would figure into West Point's memories and myth. A fortified bluff town on the eastern bank of the Mississippi, Vicksburg, with Port Hudson, Louisiana, to the south, controlled the lower Mississippi River for the Confederates. U.S. Grant, whose reputation up to this point in the war was not high and was tarnished by rumors about his drinking too much, had an army of 33,000 men

Tecumseh Sherman, who made a diversionary attack north of the city, and Admiral David Porter, who ran past the Confederate guns with his gunboat fleet, Grant crossed on April 30 with his troops. A week later Sherman's troops joined him, and the combined force set out eastward with only 120 wagons and 5 days' rations. By the time Union soldiers reached Jackson, the state capital, they had won every battle with the enemy. They then turned back toward Vicksburg, beat General Pemberton, and besieged the Confederate garrison in the city. Between April 30 and May 16 Grant's troops won five battles, took 8,000 prisoners, and closed Pemberton's army up in Vicksburg. Pemberton was besieged until July 4, when he surrendered, the day after the Battle of Gettysburg was won, making it "the best Fourth of July since 1776."

Grant's tactical genius was smoothly demonstrated at Vicksburg when he made his bold crossing of the river and his cross-country march, which separated General Pemberton at Vicksburg from the rest of the Confederate army in the area. Had he attacked the heavily fortified Vicksburg directly, the city could have been reinforced by troops coming in from the east. By separating the different parts of the Confederate Army, Grant showed that he could apply Professor Mahan's dictum: "An army that throws itself . . . between several fractions of an enemy's army beyond supporting distance of each other, may, by superior activity, defeat them all in succession." When Grant was made General in Chief of the Armies in March 1864, it was because of such tactical brilliance. His opponent Lee, of course, was also brilliant and could anticipate many of Grant's actions. Eventually, however, even with leaders equally astute on both sides, the superior numbers, resources, and industry of the North gave them such an advantage that the South was worn down and the war was won.

Wartime West Point

At West Point itself, despite the influence of the Academy and its teaching in the war, there was little connection with actual combat. After the graduations of the classes of May and June 1861, classes remained at the Academy for their full tenure. Faculty and equipment were enlisted in the war early on, but the faculty was replaced by disabled officers

camped on the west bank of the Mississippi north of Vicksburg in January 1863. After three months of skirmishing with the troops of General John C. Pemberton, Vicksburg's commander, in the bayous around the city, Grant concluded with the tenaciousness that made him great that "There was nothing left to be done but to go forward to a decisive victory."

The means of achieving this, Grant determined, was to cross the Mississippi south of Vicksburg, capture the countryside to the east, and attack the city from the rear. Aided by General William

Abner Doubleday, Class of 1842, fired the first return shot from Fort Sumter in 1861 and served throughout the Civil War, rising to major general. He gained greater fame by popularizing baseball.

after the first few battles. One of the few direct connections with the war experienced by the cadets was the visit in 1862 of President Lincoln, who came to talk to General Winfield Scott, now retired and living at West Point. The President was taken on a tour of the Napoleon Gallery, where Professor Mahan's "Napoleon Club" met and where maps of the French emperor's battles hung. The President was impressed and asked for copies of the maps; he may have more easily understood what his West Point-trained generals were doing as a consequence.

One of the few martial interruptions to the West Point routine was occasioned by the Draft Riots in New York City in the summer of 1863. There were widespread riots by the poor who resented the inequities of the draft law. Because the local militia forces had been called to resist Lee's invasion of Pennsylvania, there were no adequate forces in the city to deal with the crisis, and the garrison of enlisted men at West Point was summoned. At the same time there was a rumor that the Southern sympathizers in the North, known as "Copperheads," were organizing an attack on the Cold Spring Foundry, across the river from West Point, where Robert Parrot (Class of 1824) was manufacturing his famous Parrot gun. Superintendent Alexander Bowman armed the cadets and put them on guard duty, but no attack came. There was almost no other excitement at the Academy. Cadet Cullen Bryant had written to his father early in the war, "We are almost completely secluded and shut out from the rest of the world." And that seclusion would be maintained: in 1863, Congress voted funds to build a road north from the Academy that would make it more accessible, but the superintendent insisted that the work be stopped, writing, "It would be ruinous to the morals and discipline of the Corps [to have] an easy approach to Newburgh."

The one lasting innovation that the war brought to student life was the introduction of baseball, whose invention was popularly attributed to General Abner Doubleday (Class of 1842). The game became popular with enlisted men in the Northern armies and with the cadets who remained at West Point during the war. Baseball continued to be an active sport at West Point from that time, and before the end of the century there were intercollegiate games.

Status of the Frontier

The one place where there were active engagements for the Army after the Civil War was the frontier. There Academy graduates performed with imagination and intelligence as they had throughout the 19th century, although—as they also had earlier—they complained about the gap between formal tactical training and the fighting they actually had to do.

The first frontier engagement after the Civil War was not against the Indians as most were, but dealt with the frontier between the United States and Mexico. Napoleon III had installed Austrian Archduke Maximilian and his wife Carlota as emperor and empress of Mexico during the Civil War, thinking to set up what would essentially be a French colony in America and expecting to be able to do so unopposed if the South won the Civil War. With the defeat of the South, Napoleon found himself supporting a costly and unpopular war in Mexico against the inhabitants, a war he was almost certain to lose. The United States, newly freed to look after its borders and support the Monroe Doctrine, sent General Philip Sheridan, hero of the Shen-

One of the great innovations of Army operations on the Western plains was the use of cavalry as mounted infantry, rather than reconnaissance forces. Training at West Point prepared cadets for plains warfare through skirmish drills (above) *and horsemanship exercises* (left).

Officers' families pose outside their sod quarters (right) at Fort Sill in 1874. The bleak existence contrasted with the Eastern myth of the romantic West.

The surveying expedition of 1st Lt. George M. Wheeler, Class of 1866, seen leaving Camp Mohave, Arizona (below), surveyed west of the 100th meridian—including the area of the Grand Canyon—from 1871 until 1879.

A member of Wheeler's expedition perches (far right) on the edge of the canyon, which took the explorers one month to descend by river.

EXPEDITION OF 1871.

andoah and Petersburg campaigns, to the Mexican border with an army of 50,000 men in November 1865. Sheridan's troops, disgruntled at having their dismissal postponed, were not at all in favor of the campaign, but to the extent that they noticed it, the American people were, and the French did not know the demoralized state of Sheridan's forces. At the same time that Sheridan was deployed to the Rio Grande, General John Schofield (Class of 1853) was sent to Paris on a secret mission by Secretary of State William Seward and enjoined to "get your legs under Napoleon's mahogany and tell him he must get out of Mexico." Schofield, later to be superintendent of the Academy, was set afloat in the dip-

lomatic life of Paris by Ambassador John Bigelow. At several meetings with Napoleon III and his military officers, Schofield gave them to understand that not only was the United States opposed to any foreign power entrenching itself on Western soil, but also that United States military strength was sufficient to oppose it. His advisors impressed on Napoleon that any engagement with the Americans would be extremely costly, and on January 22, 1866, Napoleon announced the fiction that the government of Maximilian was consolidating itself and that consequently the French forces would no longer need to stay in Mexico. Within another year all French forces had been withdrawn to the utter de-

Although camping along the river (preceding page) *appeared tranquil, the trip was arduous. Once, Wheeler noted, rations were so low that there were not enough to make a pillow to sleep on.*

In the Western mountains an outpost such as Fort Garland, Colorado, had more dramatic scenery than Fort Sill, but military life still alternated between long periods of tedium and brief spells of dangerous skirmishing.

Timothy O'Sullivan's photograph "The Foot of the Grand Canyon," taken thirty-five miles below the present-day site of Hoover Dam, has been called "one of his finest views" by photography historian Beaumont Newhall.

struction of Napoleon's protégé Maximilian, but to the glory of American might, which had merely had to flex its muscles to make France take notice.

The other campaigns of those decades between the wars, on that shifting frontier between "civilization" and "Indian territory," were not so neat and were never conducted with legs "under the mahogany." General Sheridan wrote in 1868 in his yearly report as commanding general of the Army:

The Army has nothing to gain by war with the Indians; on the contrary it has everything to lose. In such a war it suffers all the hardships and privations, exposed as it is to the charge of assassination if the Indians are killed, to the charge of inefficiency if they are not; to misrepresentation by the agents who fatten on the plunder of the Indians, and misunderstood by worthy people at a distance who are deceived by these agents.

This was generally the attitude of the Army. General Sherman, despite his declared attitude that "war . . . is hell" when it was a declared war against an acknowledged enemy, believed that the Indians were being manipulated so as to be deprived of their land. In later life he regarded the work he did keeping peace with the Indians as being of more permanent worth than anything he had done during the Civil War. Nonetheless, despite the enlightened attempts of such men as Sheridan and Sherman, the march of white settlements westward across the Plains was inexorable. The conflict between settlers and Plains Indians was one unending brutal war. Between 1790 and 1898 there were sixty-nine campaigns in which thousands on both sides were killed. Between 1869 and 1876 alone, at the time of greatest conflict in the Plains, there were 200 battles.

Indian Campaigns: Northern Plains

The two great theaters of war in those years were the Northern Plains of North Dakota, Wyoming, and Montana, where the Sioux, the Blackfoot, the Crow, the Cheyenne, and the Nez Percé roamed, and the area of northern New Mexico and Arizona where the Apache, Comanche, and other tribes lived. The Sioux battled continuously for their homelands in the decade following the Civil War, but their efforts were doomed after the discovery of gold in the Black Hills of South Dakota in 1875. General Sheridan was able to keep prospectors for gold out of the Indians' homeland for one summer, but that was all; when the prospectors came through, the last and greatest pitched battles of the Sioux occurred.

The best-known figure and the great victim of these wars, on the military side at least, was Colonel George Armstrong Custer. Custer was a member of that poignant Class of 1861 at the Academy and a

George Armstrong Custer (Class of June 1861), although last in his class academically, was one of its most visible and popular members. Throughout his career Custer had a knack for being at the center of events.

popular and controversial figure from the day he got off the boat at West Point and was nicknamed "Fanny" because of his golden curls. Custer would graduate last in his class of thirty-four, but he lived in the memory of all his classmates as the greatest charmer and prankster of their time at the Academy. Morris Schaff, who described Custer as "a big jolly boy," was pulled out of bed by his heels by Custer on his first night at the Academy and became so devoted to him that he stuffed paper in his shoes to make himself tall enough to qualify for the big infantry men of "D" Company where Custer served.

The peaceful picnic setting (above), *with Custer leaning against the tent pole, disguises both the danger and the monotony of frontier life.*

Polo (right, top) *invented by the British in India and brought to America in 1876, kept cavalry skills finely honed at Fort Sill in the late 19th century.*

Arizona camp life (right) *for Army officers in 1871 was rarely as relaxed as they tried to make it appear.*

Custer's good spirits and gallantry stayed with him throughout the war and prompted such acts as his sending a message to John Pelham, CSA, a classmate who had beaten him at Fredericksburg, "I rejoice, dear Pelham, in your success." It was Custer who, as a major-general of the volunteers, harried Lee's retreating army from Richmond in April 1865 and to whom the flag of truce before Appomattox–a white towel–was brought. Sheridan later sent the towel along with the table on which Grant had written the surrender terms as a present to Custer, writing, "I know of no one whose efforts have contributed more to this happy result than those of Custer."

With his genius for being in the conspicuous place at the important moment, Custer tried to enlist in the Mexican Army of Liberation against Maximilian, but President Andrew Johnson refused his request for leave. In 1866 he was assigned to the 7th Cavalry with the rank of lieutenant colonel, and, because the first and second colonels never joined their command, Custer was in charge until his death. Because of the drama of the Little Big Horn debacle, it is not generally realized today that he had long been a controversial and heroic figure. He had been court-martialed as a scapegoat for a botched Indian campaign in 1868, less than three years after Sheridan praised him; he testified three months before his death to corruption in the Bureau of Indian Affairs, an appearance that so displeased President Grant that Custer was again temporarily deprived of his command; and in 1874 he had published a riveting account of his Western career, *My Life on the Plains*, which had quickly become a bestseller.

It will never be known exactly what happened at Little Big Horn. It appears that Custer's impetuosity and desire to reestablish his good name after President Grant's disapproval may have led him to act imprudently. It is also true, however, as General Sherman wrote in his official report for the year, that the "campaign had been planned on wrong premises" and that there had been no reason for Custer to assume that he would encounter a force significantly larger than his own.

The facts of the matter are these: Custer, returned from testifying in Washington and President Grant's displeasure, had been restored to command of his regiment on the plea of General Alfred Terry, district commander. Terry, John Gibbon (Class of 1847) with his 7th Infantry, and Custer with his 7th Cavalry were to round up all the Sioux who were harassing the whites in the Black Hills. The Sioux were under the command of Crazy Horse, a wily and accomplished chief whose well-armed and swift horsemen were the equal of the best cavalry in the world–as the United States cavalry well knew. On May 17, 1876, Terry, Gibbon, and Custer left the Missouri River to move against the Sioux. They encountered a broad Indian trail about three weeks later, and Terry decided to move west and to send Custer to locate the force that made the trail and then move south of them (at his own discretion according to the only orders that exist), thus bottling up the enemy.

Custer, with his 655 men of the 7th Cavalry, on June 25 came upon a camp that was, in fact, the entire Sioux force of 2,500 to 4,000. He had intended, it is thought, to make a surprise attack the following morning (although even in a surprise he would have been heavily outnumbered), but he realized that his troops had been sighted. Deciding on an immediate attack, he divided his troops into three battalions (remembering, perhaps, Professor Mahan's dictum to divide and attack an opposing force of superior numbers at several points?) and sent one group against the village to the left, one straight ahead, and moved to the right himself. The other two battalions were driven back to nearby bluffs that they successfully defended until the Indians left the next day, but Custer and the 265 men with him were surrounded by Indians under Crazy Horse and killed to a man. Their horses were also killed, except for one named Comanche, the sole survivor of "Custer's last stand." When the other battalions came out on the morning of the 27th, they found the 265 bodies stripped, scalped, and otherwise mutilated, except for that of Custer. His, although stripped, was untouched except for a bullet hole in the left temple and one in the left side.

Custer with his long yellow hair, his buccaneer's swagger, and his infectious high spirits that had incarnated the spirit of adventure and the romance of the cavalry for his generation, became a tragic figure overnight. The charges of recklessness and rash daring made against him only added luster

The only survivor from Custer's 7th Cavalry detachment at the Battle of Little Big Horn in 1876 was a horse named Comanche. Both Custer's career as recounted in My Life on the Plains *and his death riveted Eastern attention on the Indian wars.*

to his image. Custer, with his sensitive perceptions and generosity of spirit, had made a perceptive statement about the Indian wars some years before, writing, "If I were an Indian, I would certainly prefer to cast my lot . . . to the free and open plains rather than submit to the confined limits of a reservation, there to be the recipients of the blessed benefits of civilization with its vices thrown in."

In 1877, Crazy Horse, whom his enemies in the United States Army called "one of the bravest of the brave and one of the subtlest and most capable of captains," was defeated, after waging many campaigns on his own land as masterfully as any that had been conducted during the Civil War. Also in 1877 the Crow, the Blackfoot, the Ute, and Nez Percé were defeated or expelled from their lands. Still, in 1881, President Chester Arthur declared, "We have to deal with the appalling fact that though thousands of lives have been sacrificed and hundreds of millions of dollars expended in the attempt to solve the Indian problem, it has until within the past few years seemed scarcely nearer a solution than it was half a century ago."

Indian Campaigns: The Last Years

In the Southwest years of warfare with the Apache were brought to a close in 1886 when Geronimo, the most feared Apache chief, was captured. He became a Christian convert and settled down at Fort Sill, Oklahoma, where he grew watermelons and corn and from which he traveled to appear in Theodore Roosevelt's inaugural parade in 1905.

The man who was responsible for Geronimo's peaceful transformation into model farmer was Hugh L. Scott, Class of 1876, and later superintendent of the Academy. Scott's intellectual curiosity and brilliant diplomacy made him unique in coping with the "Indian problem." He learned their sign language so that for the first time somebody could talk to them at length and to more than one tribe. When compared with Custer's combination of flamboyance and gallantry, Scott's skills suggest how rich and varied the West Point pool of talent was. Hugh Scott had graduated from the Academy just a few weeks after Custer was killed, and he joined the 7th Cavalry. Intellectually curious, he began to study the Sioux language, hoping to arbitrate with the newly defeated Sioux and other tribes. He discovered, how-

Field artillery (preceding page), *drawn up in the Montana snow, waits expectantly during the 1876–1877 Wolf Mountain campaign against the Sioux.*

A poignant footnote to the daring and grandeur of the Indian defense of their land was the residence at Fort Sill for his last twenty years of the subdued Apache chief Geronimo (below), shown here displaying pumpkins he has grown.

The Sioux camp (left) at the Pine Ridge Agency, South Dakota, appears tranquil in 1891, but only a few months earlier the last clash with the Army had occurred at Wounded Knee.

The 10th Infantry stands for inspection at Fort Sill in 1897 (below), a time when frontier duty has been called "as routine as death, taxes, and mess-call."

ever, that a spoken language was good for only one tribe but that sign language such as the Indians had refined for generations was good for communication among many tribes and was, in fact, known to be the language of arbitration.

Scott became a familiar and trusted arbitrator throughout the Plains and the Southwest and was valuable in that office for the next twenty years. It was his persuasiveness that turned Geronimo into a farmer at Fort Sill, a post that even cavalry officers often found stultifying and where homesteaders found farming backbreaking. And it was Scott who, traveling from tribe to tribe, kept the "Ghost Dance" revival of 1890 from developing into a full-fledged rebellion, although even he could not prevent the last confrontation at Wounded Knee, a massacre that signaled the end of conflict between the Indians and the white man. Nonetheless, Scott's innovations in communication and skills in peacemaking were as valuable in spanning the gap between white and Indian needs as were Custer's sentimentality or General Sheridan's skills in furthering the white man's advantage.

"Old Bentz" (right), *the West Point bugler through much of the 19th century, was a much beloved local character. All of the changes in the routine of a cadet's day were announced by bugle.*

CADET LIFE: THE
QUIET YEARS

uster's flamboyance and Scott's quiet versatility were only two aspects of the varied character that West Point instilled in its graduates. Despite the emphasis at the Academy on uniformity of behavior and the insistence, come down from Thayer's day, that each cadet was equal to the other, any place accruing the almost mythic significance that West Point assumed throughout the 19th century was bound to have its share of personal traditions. By the Civil War there were many military families that had representatives in at least two generations at West Point and sometimes three. One family that served conspicuously and tragically in this way were the Meigses. Montgomery Cunningham Meigs, Class of 1836, the son of a Philadelphia doctor, served in the engineer corps for twenty-five years after his graduation with great success and satisfaction to himself. One of the projects he oversaw was the Washington Aqueduct, which carried water from the falls of the Potomac to the city of Washington. On two successive days in 1861 he was appointed colonel and then brigadier general, and he served through the war as quartermaster-general of the United States Army. James E. Blaine, presidential candidate of the 1880s, remarked of Meigs's tenure as quartermaster-general: "One of the ablest graduates of the Military Academy, [he] was kept from the command of troops by the inestimably important services he performed as Quartermaster-General. . . . Perhaps in the military history of the world there was never so large an amount of money disbursed upon the order of a single man. . . . The aggregate sum could not have been less during the war than fifteen hundred millions of dollars, accurately vouched and accounted for to the last cent."

While Meigs was serving so ably, his son, John Rodgers Meigs, was a cadet. The Academy was virtually untouched by the war directly (once the Southerners had left in 1861), and its pastoral seclusion is suggested by a photograph of the Class of 1863 in which young Meigs was first. The cadets lounge in the photograph a little stiffly, a little self-consciously, against a granite wall. Trees are in full leaf behind them, and they are framed by the classical pillars of the old academic building to the left and a gas lamp post to the right—symbols of the classical tradition and enlightenment. The one class member whose attitude seems not to be determined

John Rodgers Meigs, Class of 1863, kneels, front row center, with his class. He was killed less than a year later, and Secretary of War Stanton noted: "One of the . . . brightest ornaments of the military profession, he has fallen a victim to murderous rebel warfare."

The Civil War's personal drama was particularly acute for families with a tradition of West Point service. Brig. Gen. Montgomery Meigs, Class of 1836, Quartermaster-General of the Union Army, lost his son John (left) late in the war.

88

Despite the informality of sports, this cadet crew on the Hudson (above) in the 1870s remains serious and retains a military bearing.

Perched at the base of Battle Monument (left), dedicated to the officers and enlisted man of the Regular Army killed in the Civil War, two cadets and a young belle enjoy an early summer day.

exclusively by the presence of the camera is young Meigs, who hunkers down, alone in the line of his comrades, almost as though he is trying to avoid being exceptional. Less than a year after his graduation, John Rodgers Meigs was killed in Virginia. Secretary of War Edwin Stanton wrote: "One of the youngest and brightest ornaments of the military profession, he has fallen a victim to murderous rebel warfare."

The sobering death of Lieutenant Meigs did not stop the family tradition of military service. Two namesakes of the quartermaster-general were graduated in the 20th century and one, like John Rodgers Meigs, lost his life soon after graduation.

The death of family members and the brutality of the division of the war scarcely dispelled the aura of the military academy as a unique and special hollowing of a man's life, however, to judge by the fact that such Confederate generals as James Longstreet, Class of 1842; Simon Bolivar Buckner, Class of 1844; and John B. Hood, Class of 1853, had sons or grandsons registered at the Academy within a few years after the end of war. The depth of loyalty

Nellie Dent Sharp, whose mother was a sister of U.S. Grant's wife, often attended the summer hops at West Point and saved her dance programs (above and right). She eventually married John Bradbury Bennet, Class of 1891, her frequent dance partner.

West Point engendered is suggested by the fact that, of course, the descendants of the Confederates were classmates of the sons of such United States Army generals as John Pope, Grant, and Sheridan.

The Post-War Scene

With the end of the war traditions—no matter how benign—hardened and the bucolic atmosphere at West Point deepened. The cadets marched and drilled in summer camp, carrying bookcases into wooden floored tents in which they were supposed to learn field tactics and flirting at "hops" attended by the most eligible young ladies from Boston and New York. A small blue-backed book published in 1867 for visitors and prospective cadets and called *Guide to West Point and the U.S. Military Academy* waxes lyrical about the social life and high jinks of summer camp:

> *The presence of visitors contributes much to enliven this period of hardship in Cadet life, and the tri-weekly dancing parties on Monday, Wednesday, and Friday evenings, notwithstanding their abrupt termination at 10 P.M., affords never to be forgotten reminiscences in after life, of social enjoyment and enlightened intercourse with the fair daughters of America, not a few of whom date back their after career to the bewitching influence which marks this season. . . . An illumination of the camp usually takes place on the evening before it is broken up, and the convolutions of a 'stag dance' are performed on the Parade-ground, with a fervor and vivacity worthy of imitation in a Camanche war-dance. This curious cross in the terpsichorean art, between the pigeon wing, double shuffle, hoe-down, and the quadrille, is a frequent diversion in the Cadet camp. It is performed by twenty or more Cadets, who gyrate between two rows of candles stuck in the ground, cadencing their movements by the very uncertain sounds of a plebian fiddle and the low muffled rattle of a drum, accompanied by whimsicalities and contortions unknown save at West Point.*

The Academy was the favorite resort and object of attention of the Army's senior staff. General Sher-

Miss Sharp

SERIES OF HOPS

Camp R.S.MacKenzie

July 15 - 1889 -

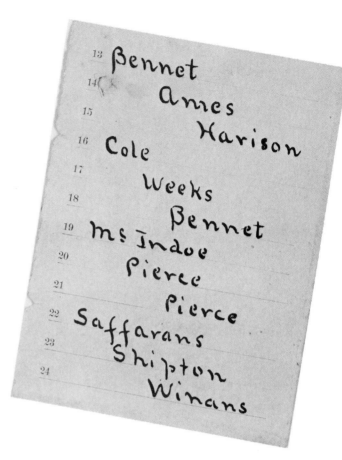

13 Bennet
14 Ames
15 Harison
16 Cole
17 Weeks
18 Bennet
19 McIndoe
20 Pierce
21 Pierce
22 Saffarans
23 Shipton
24 Winans

JOHN BRADBURY BENNET

COLONEL U.S. INFANTRY

man visited West Point repeatedly during the years that he was commander in chief of the Army (1869–1883) and dispensed such advice as, "My boy, if you have not yet picked out your girl, wait! They'll be all the prettier, next year!" He also had a habit of overruling the superintendent's disciplinary sentences on cadets, giving such reasons as, "In my day we always cut up on 'New Year's Eve' and the custom has a tacit recognition. . ." In 1881 former President and Mrs. Grant made a surprise visit to commencement during General Sherman's speech, and they modestly refused to take a seat on the platform although they remained the objects of affectionate regard of all at the ceremony.

The Academic Regime

While inventiveness and adaptability characterized many of the Academy's graduates, and while the holocaust of the Civil War with its total devastation had revolutionized warfare, the Academy, in both academic and social life, remained unchanged. The institution that had directed the course of the Civil War through the skill and intelligence of its graduates ironically remained unaffected by the war, and, in fact, began to ossify. During the post Civil War period, historian and West Point chronicler Stephen Ambrose points out, American colleges ceased to be the institutions of classical learning that they had been earlier, from which gentlemen derived an education in Greek and Latin designed to enhance their leisure, and became repositories of all branches of knowledge. Students were encouraged to choose a course of study, instead of being guided through a single classical curriculum. Specialists were turned out of these colleges and even more specialized graduate schools were set up to turn the undergraduate major into a professional. West Point alone of the major American universities did nothing to adapt to this development.

Some of the changes wrought in the history of warfare by the Civil War included the tactical changes of using cavalry as mounted infantry—an innovation useful in the West where the mounted Indians functioned in this way; despoiling the resources of the civilian population so that the enemy could not live off the land; the technical advance of the telegraph; and many improvements in artillery. At West Point, however, none of these changes was

The post-Civil War faculty (preceding page) *became entrenched—top-hatted Henry Lane Kendrick taught for 45 years—and opposed change.*

Field conditions prevailed in 1905 as cadets set up their own tents (right).

Cadets form up in 1898 in front of the old barracks (far right), *designed for Superintendent Delafield.*

One of the most colorful elements of West Point life was the band (below).

POST BAND

acknowledged. When a Civil War veteran cadet tried to explain to Professor Mahan, now in his fourth decade of teaching, why he had given an answer according to his experience rather than answering according to the text, the irascible old professor yelled at him, "I don't care what you did or what you saw during the Civil War, you stick to the text." Germany's use of many of the new weapons and skills first tried in the Civil War in their own Franco-Prussian War of 1870–1871 made that country the leader in military science. The Army sent men to Berlin to learn about the latest in German warfare. At West Point, however, the Academic Board refused to add German to the curriculum, retaining French, the language of Napoleon, and Spanish, which had come in after the Mexican War.

The faculty's entrenched interest encouraged the maintenance of the status quo. Faculty members

ruled the school through the Academic Board and considered the recommendations of short-tenured superintendents if they wanted to and ignored them if they did not. Unlike the faculty first gathered by Sylvanus Thayer, which came from outside the Army and outside the country as well, the post Civil War instructors were almost all West Point graduates who had settled in for careers of fifteen, twenty-five, or even forty years. Promising graduates were notified by department heads when a vacancy appeared in the faculty, and they returned from a mere four or five years on duty to spend the rest of their lives at sylvan West Point, far removed from any theaters of conflict. Although they conscientiously enough taught the mathematics and rather dated engineering that had been innovative in the 1830s and 1840s, it bore less and less relation to modern military practice. West Point had always been accused of being theoretical rather than practical; now even the theory was not sound. Such professors as Edward Edgar Wood, professor of French 1892–1910, who did not speak or read French but only taught grammar, and Henry Lane Kendrick, who taught at West Point from 1835 to 1880, represent the extreme of persnickety pedagogical practice and long service, but they were by no means atypical.

The 1867 *Guide to West Point* describes the rigid classroom procedure that had frozen Thayer's system of small sections into what were as much exercises in deportment as exercises in learning. The *Guide* asserts that:

> *The Academic Exercises of the Cadets are not devoid of interest even to those who are attracted to the spot by the glittering displays of military life.... Each class is divided into convenient sections of from twelve to fifteen*

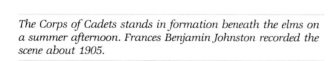

The Corps of Cadets stands in formation beneath the elms on a summer afternoon. Frances Benjamin Johnston recorded the scene about 1905.

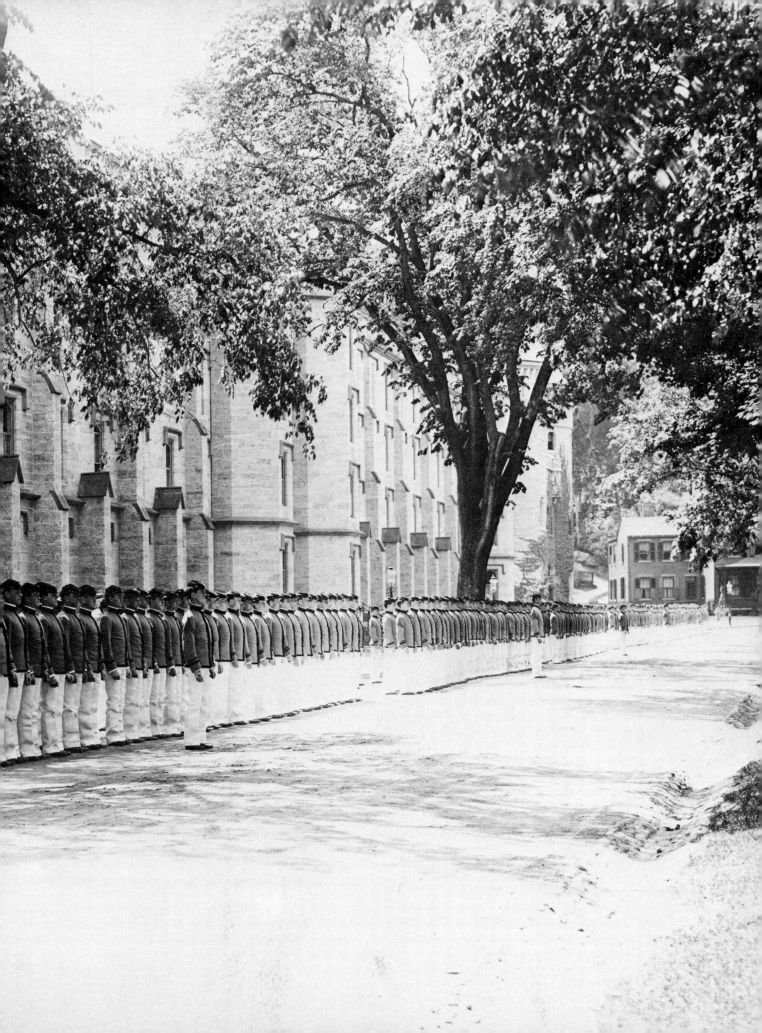

Cadets ... the first Cadet on each section roll being its squad-marcher, and being responsible for its punctual attendance and deportment. The recitation hours are sounded on a bugle, when the sections for the hour are formed at the Barracks, their rolls are called, and they are marched to the Recitation-rooms by their several squad-marchers.... [a cadet] being called on, first enunciates the proposition to be discussed, then gives a condensed analysis of how it should be solved, and then gives full discussion, delineation, or demonstration with reference to his diagram or analysis.... It is a matter of no small magnitude to secure a becoming personal deportment and style in recitation, and to suppress the unmeaning, nervous turnings, rockings, and fumblings, which too often deform the manners of undisciplined students.

Critics of the Academy

There were critics. Lieutenant Elmer Hubbard, who had taught chemistry at West Point from 1889 to 1893, wrote an article criticizing the teaching methods and curriculum, while Senator John Logan of Illinois, who had harbored a grudge against the Academy ever since the Civil War, when he had been passed over for promotion in favor of West Point men, wrote a book charging that West Point had created a military oligarchy. General John Schofield, Civil War veteran, diplomat, and former superintendent of the Academy, called for a more well-rounded curriculum when he was president of the Board of Visitors in 1901. Morris Schaff in the midst of his reminiscences of Custer and cadet high jinks in *The Spirit of Old West Point* pauses to note that there has been a "decline in the importance of military engineering [and while] it is true that the great advance in gun construction, and in applied science for their effective use, makes a much greater demand for scientific knowledge than formerly existed.... to supply this knowledge is the basis and aim of all technical schools; and, besides, it has become a necessary and well-established feature of all large steel and shipbuilding works. However great may hitherto have been the dependence of the government on its graduates at West Point for the proper adaptation of scientific knowledge to its defense, under present conditions that dependence must be much less. Therefore a change giving the graduate wider knowledge in the suggestive fields of history and literature might well be considered."

All criticisms fell on deaf ears, however. The accusation that West Point men did not know how to conduct practical warfare had been so handsomely disproven by their conduct in the Civil War that the Academy considered that argument answered for all time. The argument that they should be equipped to lead civilian armies was, despite Jefferson's hope that that very leadership would justify the Academy's existence, something that had always been resisted by the Regular Army. In fact, at the beginning of the Civil War, General Winfield Scott made any Regular Army officer who wanted to lead volunteers resign from the Regular Army first. The idea that the curriculum should be broadened in the humanities was countered with the observation that such a change would certainly not make more practical Army men. In 1917 a visiting alumnus noted, "The great charm of West Point is that so many things never change." From the end of the Civil War until that date this was true.

One of the few areas where any change was noted was in cadet life, which became at once more restricted officially and much rougher unofficially. As evidence of the generally torpid growth of the school, the number of cadets increased only from 220 in 1843 to 492 in 1900, and for the most part the cadet of 1900 lived very much as his counterpart a half century before had, even to using the same slang. In some ways for the cadet of the later 19th century, despite improved transportation and communications, life was even more limited, however. Smoking, which had been a popular pastime in the cadets' rooms, was outlawed completely; and such illegal but affectionately regarded haunts as Benny Havens's tavern just off the post had closed down. The Victorian Sabbath that blanketed the western world had driven out frontier virtues and energy that made cadets of the 1820s and 1830s dare risks such as the young Jefferson Davis did when he broke a leg returning one dark night from Benny Havens's. There were certain official ways to let off steam that had been added to the program after the Civil War.

Henry Ossian Flipper, Class of 1877 and the Academy's first black graduate, was generally ostracized at West Point and had a difficult Army career. The few 19th century black cadets were usually ignored, a treatment more extensive than plebe year hazing.

One was the clowning and lampooning of 100th Night, which took place one hundred days before graduation and in which the second classmen made up skits that made fun of the graduating first classmen. But the real substitute for the carrying on of earlier times was hazing.

The Role of Hazing

Before the Civil War hazing, or submitting the incoming fourth classmen to pranks intended as an initiation rite, had been quite mild. They took place in summer camp, to which the plebes reported di-

99

rectly, and were no more severe than any modern youngster who has been away to camp may know. The change came in 1865 when the age of admission was raised to twenty-four, and Civil War veterans—some with full beards—were admitted as plebes. Determined not to be outfaced, the upperclassmen who were in charge of conditioning the plebes instituted much more severe hazing. The practice of "bracing" or standing at exaggerated attention for long periods of time; the assignment of impossible tasks; the harassing of plebes at meals; and the forcing of rope ends, soap, quinine, and tabasco sauce on plebes for food characterized hazing at its worst. The system had its defenders, who claimed that it promoted cool-headedness and implicit obedience to orders, and it had its critics, among them most of the superintendents who simply pointed out that it was illegal under the regulations. Despite the departure from the ideal of Colonel Thayer's day of each cadet being equal but also *equally a gentleman*, hazing stayed. Many of the alumni who had gone through their own hazing regarded it sentimentally from the distance of the years, and most of the plebes felt that it would make men of them and that, in any case, it was the rankest dishonor to inform on fellow cadets. When there were com-

plaints—sometimes from parents—the superintendents never could get the injured cadet to agree that he had been harmed. In 1902, Cadet Oscar Booz had been severely hazed by being forced to drink tabasco sauce with every meal; he eventually resigned, only to die within a year from an injured larynx. At the same time Douglas MacArthur, the object of special hazing because of the prominence of his father, General Arthur MacArthur, went into convulsions after having been forced to do spread eagles, a type of deep knee bend. Booz had complained, but MacArthur resisted Congressional suggestions of harm.

Cadet activities ranged from billiards (left), a recreation appropriate to a gentleman's leisure time, to pranks at summer camp when plebes were required to perform absurd stunts, such as a funeral for a rat (above).

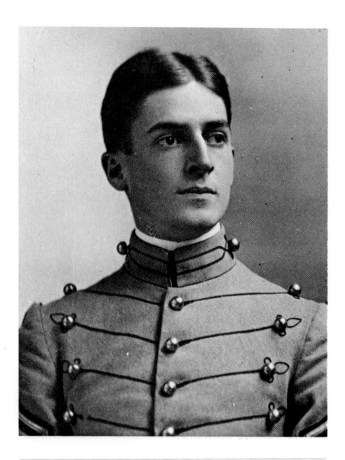

Upperclassmen severely hazed Cadet Douglas MacArthur, Class of 1903, because of the prominence of his father, Maj. Gen. Arthur MacArthur, commander in the Philippines.

Baseball and Football

One innovation in the program of induction that particularly encouraged hazing was the introduction of a three-week training camp for plebes. Known as "Beast Barracks," the three weeks were characterized more by hazing than by any formal instruction. One result of the more severe hazing, of course, was that when plebes became third classmen at the end of their first year, they were so relieved and had invested so much in their initiation, that the sense of belonging to a unique group was all the more marked.

The only other way of letting off energy that was introduced to West Point during the period between the Civil War and the Spanish-American War was the introduction of intercollegiate sports. These, of course, also did much toward ending West Point's Olympian isolation. Football, which had begun as an adaptation of rugby and become popular at Princeton, Rutgers, and other eastern colleges in the 1870s, was not well known at West Point until Dennis Mahan Michie, the son of one old West Point professor and the namesake of another, played it at prep school and then came to West Point as a cadet. Eager to play at the Academy, Michie had some friends at Annapolis send West Point a challenge and then went to his father, Peter Smith Michie, the head of the Academic Board but a doting

parent, to get permission. Army lost that first game in the fall of 1890, 24 to 0. Inflamed, the Academy returned the challenge the next year and won, 32 to 16. The great tradition introduced by Dennis Michie (who would die in the Spanish-American War less than a decade later) was one of the most vigorous products of the Academy, although Army did not play Navy from 1894 to 1897 because feelings about the game had run so high. Michie's contribution to West Point tradition was permanently recognized when the Academy named its football stadium in his honor.

Baseball, which had been played sporadically ever since the Civil War, was officially recognized

Baseball began to be played at the Academy during the Civil War, when it was widespread among Union soldiers. By the turn of the century, there were regular intercollegiate games.

103

The popularity of athletic contests between classes and with other colleges made them a social occasion, as at this 1907 track meet.

as an extracurricular sport with class teams in the 1880s. Baseball has a special connection with West Point because the game was popularized by Abner Doubleday, Class of 1842, who was a defender at Fort Sumter in 1861 and who emerged from the Civil War as a major general. In 1891 the indefatigable Navy challenged Army at baseball but was promptly put in its place with a score of Army 4, Navy 3.

A ballcarrier rushes in the 1907 Army-Navy game. Army lost the first game between the service academies in 1890, 24 to 0.

The Legacy of Stability

With the introduction of football and baseball, counteracting the rather destructive energy that went into hazing, the significant changes in West Point life in the years after the Civil War came to an end. The stability of the routine on the Plain above the river and the rather stilted educational process would continue in the same pattern right up to the superintendency of Douglas MacArthur in 1919. The hallowed nature of the West Point that had won the Civil War and that was regarded with

awe by the American people as the spiritual birth-place of Grant, Sherman, Jackson, and Lee was reinforced by the appearance of the cadets, fresh as paint and sharp as a bayonet, at many national festivals and occasions in the 1880s and 1890s. The cadets marched at the Centennial of Washington's inauguration in New York in 1889; they were part of General Sherman's funeral in St. Louis in 1891; they went to the Chicago exposition of 1893; and they camped out in a dazzling white tent city at the St. Louis exposition of 1904. The Civil War had been the first war to be extensively photographed, and the practice of recording national events and institutions with the camera has left a complete picture of the West Point of the end of the 19th century.

Cadets were much in demand for public occasions, and in 1893 they went to the Chicago World's Fair (above), setting up camp in a white tent city that rivaled the "City Beautiful" architecture of the fair itself.

The West Point Cadets attended the St. Louis Exposition (left) in 1904 in full dress uniforms.

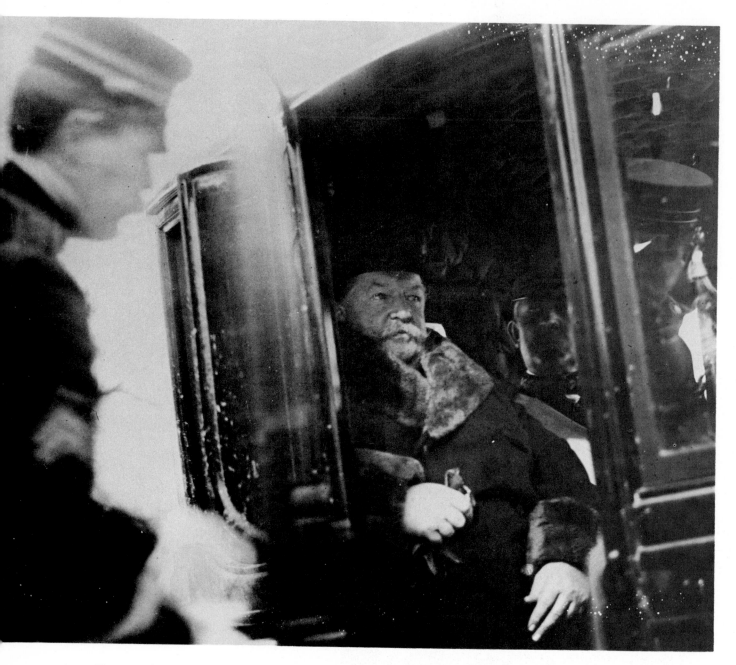

Secretary of War William Howard Taft, with all his vast presence, was bundled into a carriage in February 1908 during one of his many official visits to the Academy, both as Secretary and later as President.

Even as it seems immutable, however, that quiet West Point was, as always, a breeding ground for military genius and creativity. John J. Pershing was a graduate of the Class of 1886; Douglas MacArthur was a member of the Class of 1903; George Patton was a member of the Class of 1909; Dwight D. Eisenhower, Omar Bradley, and James Van Fleet graduated in 1915. The American efforts in World War I and World War II would be directed by West Point men. Before these global conflicts, the Spanish-American War, the Panama Canal, and the Mexican border campaign drew heavily on their spirit and intelligence.

At the West Point graduation reception in 1911, George Washington Goethals (left), Class of 1880, then chief engineer of the Panama Canal, posed with Maj. Gen. Thomas H. Barry, Class of 1877, the Academy's superintendent.

As after the Civil War, there was an ironic discrepancy after World War I between West Point's prestige and the school's curriculum, which was antiquated. Distinguished visitors were a result of the prestige and in 1919 the Prince of Wales (left) toured West Point with Academy officials.

In 1908, looking north toward the Hudson Highlands from the old fortifications of Fort Putnam, West Point's importance as a military post was still apparent.

Cadet Life: A Portfolio

The West Point experience stamped indelibly the lives of those who participated. The common bond extended first to classmates, the young men with whom a cadet spent the four years leading to commencement. After graduation, the bond expanded to include all Academy graduates, the brother officers met during long years on the frontier or at posts overseas. The basics of cadet life changed relatively little from the Civil War until after World War I, so memories were similar. Although cadets shared certain qualities—similar education, a disciplined life, and training for leadership—their backgrounds varied widely. Some cadets came from the most prominent families in America, while others had grown up in modest circumstances. West Point brought out their best characteristics by putting them through the program shown on the following pages.

Newly-arrived plebes still in civilian clothes are taught the rudiments of saluting and standing at attention in 1905.

Plebes

Before the Civil War entering plebes went directly into summer camp but after the war, as a means of tightening discipline on veterans who were sometimes older than the upperclassmen in camp, a three-week induction period known as "Beast Barracks" was instituted. Conducted largely by cadets rather than faculty and distinguished by the introduction of severe hazing, "Beast Barracks" was a controversial means of instilling discipline in the plebes and molding the class into a unified body that had survived a common experience.

Wearing their new uniforms, plebes hurry to their next task after drawing their bedding and equipment.

An upperclassman puts a squad of plebes (below) through a close-order drill exercise.

The Curriculum

The formality of classroom instruction reflected the military nature of other aspects of cadet life. Cadets were expected to recite each day, and the uniformity of the curriculum allowed cadets to compare themselves with their classmates. Other aspects of the curriculum included laboratory sessions for the practical application of engineering theory and regular physical exercise.

Cadets demonstrate parts of speech on the blackboard during English, until 1908 part of the Department of Modern Languages.

Drawing class, teaching cadets how to draft maps and sketches of terrain and fortifications, had been an integral part of the curriculum from the Academy's first days.

During an engineering class in the Academy's Department of Ordnance and Gunnery, cadets worked with various devices in the Instrument House.

In an engineering lab (below left) *cadets study structural elements that will be applied later in military bridge building. Testing supply vehicles* (far right) *on the model bridges was another element of the course.*

A "section marcher" (center left) reports in his Civil and Military Engineering class. The section system, whereby cadets were divided into small groups who studied together according to ability and performance, was one of Sylvanus Thayer's most enduring legacies.

(Preceding pages) *Learning in unison extended from physical exercises such as rope climbing and calisthenics to the gentleman's pursuits of fencing and dancing.*

The service areas of the Academy, including the laundry for the cadets (above), *were recorded in the comprehensive photographs made for West Point's centennial.*

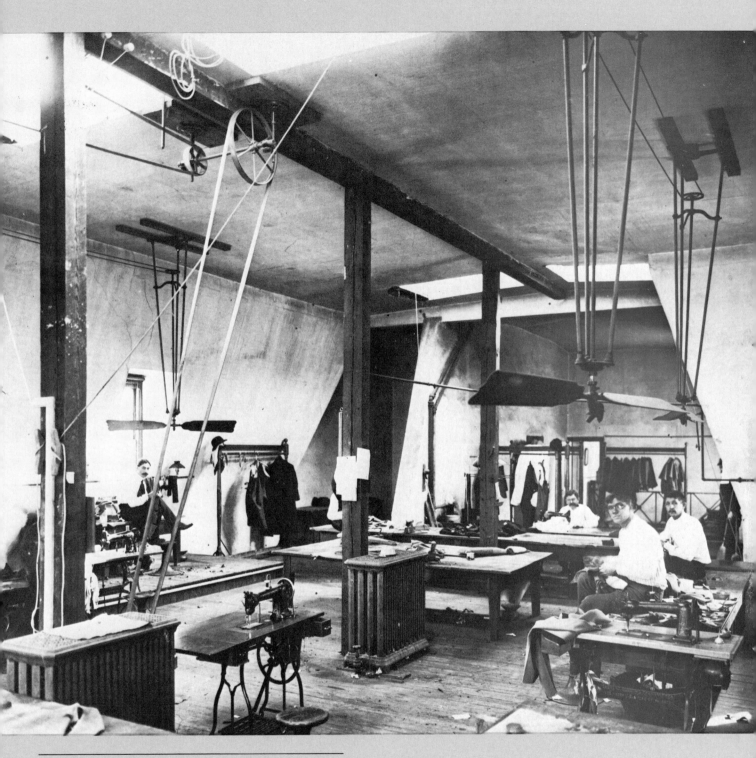

The tailor shop, where the "cadet gray" uniforms were made, was equipped with the most modern steam radiators (by the pillars) and sewing machines.

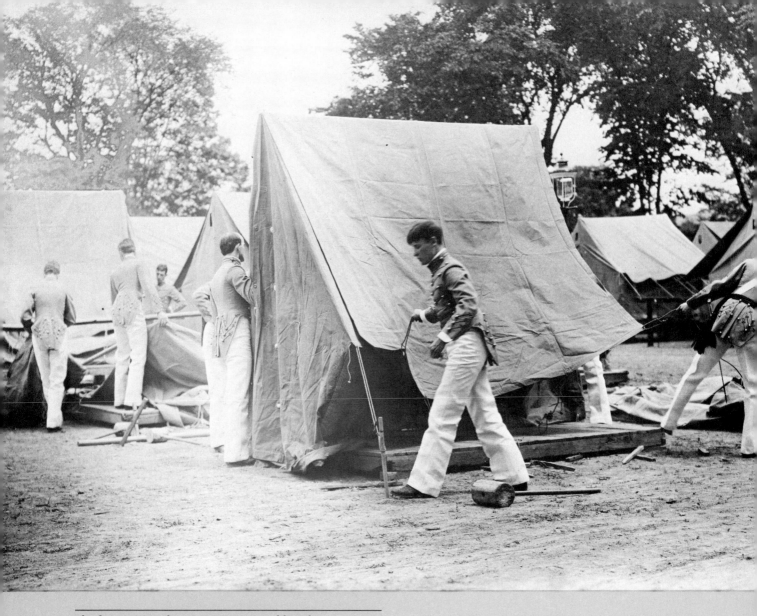

The first activity of summer camp, assembling the tent city, required cadets not only to set up their own tent but to line it up correctly with its neighbors.

Summer Camp

Summer camp, begun in 1819, started at the end of June and lasted until the end of August. All the cadets, except for those between their second and third years who went home for a two-month furlough, encamped in a tent city to the west of Fort Clinton. *The Guide to West Point* from 1867 describes it as a period "of unusual interest and hilarity. . . . The Encampment consists of eight rows of tents, two to each company, opening on four streets parallel to each other, and a broad avenue runs through the center of the camp. . . ." The physical appearance of the camp changed little through the decades, and many of the activities and drills remained identical into the 20th century.

Summer camp regulations for cadet dress and personal appearance were not in any way relaxed but conditions were hardly primitive.

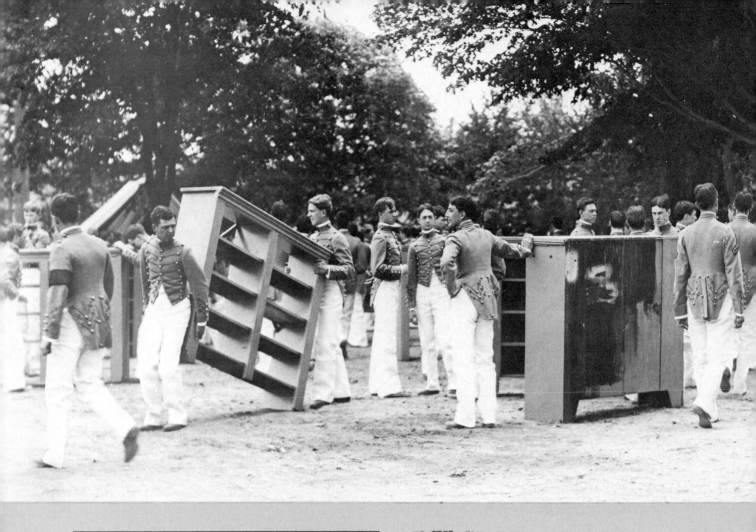

Summer camp was quite civilized, despite its aim of teaching cadets about field conditions. With rifles and equipment stacked neatly (right), cadets move bookcases into a tent in 1905.

Cadets mill around informally (left), collecting tent furnishings. Noted photographer Frances Benjamin Johnston captured the camp's idyllic quality remembered so fondly by alumni.

A parade ground formation, framed by elms, epitomizes the formal discipline and strength of the Academy, qualities that appealed to America after the Civil War.

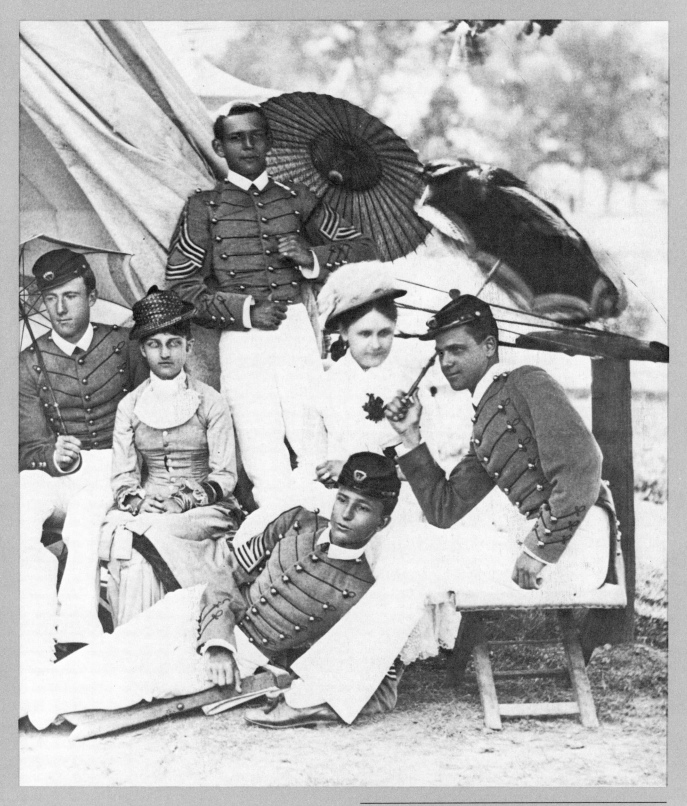

Stalwarts of the Class of 1881 socialize in summer camp. Cadets Biddle (left), Greble (standing), and Hodges (lying) became major generals.

The end of summer camp (right) marked a change in the pace of Academy life, a return to the barracks and classrooms. In August 1900, "A" Company decorated its street to celebrate the end of camp.

Military Training and Drills

Practical training ranged from individual skills such as horsemanship and riflery to cooperative exercises such as artillery and cavalry drills. Field applications of classroom theory received more emphasis as the Academy entered the 20th century.

Surveying, essential for building fortifications and roads, was part of the field training recorded in a comprehensive photographic study of West Point in 1903.

A cadet horseman learns to jump in the riding school. Until after World War I horsemanship and cavalry training were key aspects of the West Point program.

A cadet standardbearer (overleaf) *leads a cavalry formation at the Academy.*

On guard duty (overleaf right), *sentries had to challenge all who passed, which could mean offending an upperclassman if a plebe challenged too rigorously.*

At riflery practice cadets fire at distant targets (above), *which are then lowered into a trench by fellow cadets (left) so each marksman's score can be tallied.*

Cadets operate large artillery guns (above) for coastal defense. The War Department regularly sent new weapons to West Point for trial during the summer camp maneuvers.

In the summer of 1894, battery drill in white dress uniforms (preceding page) contributed to the cadets' active field training. Later, field drills more closely approximated combat conditions.

West Point cavalrymen, accompanied by gun carriages, wheel in clouds of dust on the Plain about 1900. The Old West Point Hotel is in the background.

Bridge Building

West Point was ideally situated for training cadets in bridge building. The Hudson River provided ample shoreline and sufficient current for bridges to be a challenge for novice engineers. During their later careers, when many cadets would serve in the Army's Corps of Engineers, they would be called upon to construct various types of bridges in treacherous terrain or under combat conditions. At the Academy, racing against cadet rivals taught the bridge builders to work efficiently under stress.

Bridge building was an essential practical engineering skill in the days before motorized transportation and amphibious craft. Cadet companies competed in pontoon bridge building, with the losers tossed into the Hudson.

Graduation

Graduation in June followed the annual examination of the undergraduates by the Board of Visitors. From ill-at-ease civilians introduced immediately into Beast Barracks, the cadets had been transformed in four years into disciplined, proficient soldiers, ready for a career of leadership. Commencement was a gala and impressive celebration with the Secretary of War, military personnel, and sometimes the President of the United States attending. Other festivities extended over several days, including a reception on the superintendent's lawn.

Graduating cadets, resplendent in fresh uniforms, are welcomed into the United States Army as officers.

A graduate stands proudly with his mother, politely holding her fan and purse. An Army career usually took graduates far from West Point and their classmates, but officers retained their affection for both.

Graduates, their families, Army officers, and distinguished visitors gather (above) for the customary superintendent's reception in 1905.

Horace Porter (right), Class of 1860, former Ambassador to France and President of the Association of Graduates, speaks at graduation.

A beaming Secretary of War William Howard Taft presents a diploma to a graduate in 1908. Taft frequently visited the Academy.

147

WEST POINT AND
THE WORLD

In 1898, Thomas Lafayette Rosser, a drop-out from the May Class of 1861, former major general in the Confederate Army, and former chief engineer of the Northern Pacific Railroad, was given a commission as brigadier general of the United States Army to fight in the war with Spain. Rosser, Custer's West Point roommate and cavalry opponent in the Civil War, was one of three West Pointers who became Confederate generals and who then returned to the Army during the Spanish-American War. There was also Fitzhugh Lee, Class of 1856, nephew of Robert E. Lee, a very popular instructor at the Academy when the Civil War broke out, who had resigned with regret, been serenaded by his fellow officers, and then fought gallantly with his cavalry up until some of the last battles in the war. Joe Wheeler, Class of 1859, had commanded the cavalry that offered the only impediment to Sherman's march through Georgia. In 1898 these men led the return of the South, in spirit, into the U.S. Army.

There were some mutterings: one old Confederate veteran in Alabama is recorded as saying, "I'm a Confederate and a Christian, and I always aimed to live right so's I'd go to Heaven. . . . Now I reckon I'd ruther go to Hell an' see the Devil rip them blue coats off Tom Rosser and Fitz Lee." But for most of the country—and certainly for most West Point graduates—the sentiment more nearly matched that of the contemporary chronicler who, speaking of this time when Joseph Wheeler "burst from the ashes of the Confederacy," went on to wonder "whether there ever was deeper joy than that of Wheeler, Rosser, and Fitz Lee, when once more they put on the blue uniform and drew their swords for their united country."

The return of the Confederate veterans to the Army was as much a tribute to the loyalty inculcated in West Point classmates as it was to loyalty inspired by a returned allegiance to the United States. In the years after the Civil War, West Point, despite its calcifying academics, continued to mold men into an almost indissoluble corps with common memories and a common allegiance.

Following the conquest of Cuba in the Spanish-American War, Spain's General Custellano left Havana (above) *on January 1, 1899, escorted by American troops.*

A long line of cavalry (preceding page) *patrols the border with Mexico in 1914.*

The Spanish colonial church in Malolos comes under American bombardment during the campaign against Emilio Aguinaldo's rebels.

War With Spain

The Spanish-American War, 1898–1899, was not a very distinguished testing ground of these skills and commitments but it did show, as usual, that West Point-trained leaders functioned superbly during conflict. The war itself, initiated by a jingoistic Congress with the blessing of a Republican party that wished to draw attention away from the fiscal problems of the gold standard, actually commenced after the mining of the American battleship *Maine* in Havana harbor on February 15, 1898. Spain had already indicated its willingness for peace at virtually any price when the eager Americans were confirmed in their desire for war by the explosion of the *Maine*. It is thought today that the *Maine* was probably blown up by Cuban rebels who needed American help to prosecute their own war against Spain. Following the declaration of war in April, a naval blockade of Cuba was instituted by the American fleet. Regular and volunteer U. S. Army troops landed in late June and by mid-July the Spanish in Cuba were vanquished.

John J. Pershing (front row, second from right), advanced from captain to brigadier general during his Philippine service (left).

An American officer and his aide (below) advance cautiously through the Philippine jungle.

Successes in the Pacific theater were even more spectacular. On May 1, one week after war was declared, Commodore George Dewey steamed into Manila Bay and annihilated the Spanish fleet. Dewey then asked Washington for 5,000 ground troops and while waiting for their arrival maintained a naval blockade. There was also a native rebellion in progress against the Spanish in the Philippines, and the Germans had colonial aspirations there. Urged by Kipling to "take up the White Man's burden," the Americans routed the Spanish in the Philippines and formally purchased the territory for $20 million. The guerrilla leader Emilio Aguinaldo and various insurgent tribes resented the American presence, and clashes between U.S. troops and Filipino insurgents occurred as early as February 1899. Fierce fighting was commonplace until 1902 and was marked by atrocities on both sides, including the torture and decapitation of Capt. Thomas Connell, Class of 1894.

Building even a simple bridge (above) *in the Philippine jungle forced Army engineers to depart from classroom exactness.*

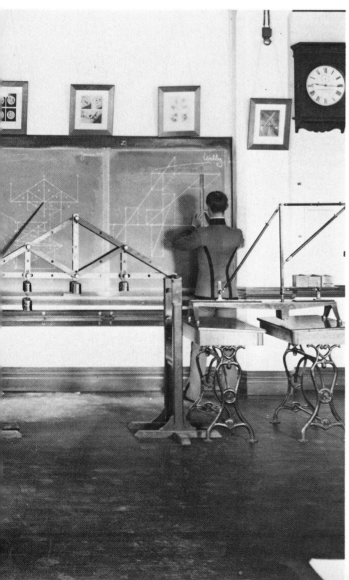

A photograph of a West Point engineering class about 1902 (left) and a view of one of the Army's bridges in the Philippines (above), about 1899, demonstrate clearly the importance of engineering in successful military campaigns and the precision with which Academy lessons were carried out in the field.

A seemingly flimsy pontoon bridge (above) could be built quickly and still support heavy equipment.

Capt. William Sibert (left), Class of 1884, applied engineering knowledge gained in the Philippines to the Panama Canal.

Officers of the China Relief Expedition (right), sent to help subdue the Boxer Rebellion in 1900, stand under a Chinese umbrella of State to accept surrender.

U.S. Engineer Office
China Relief Expedition
Photo by
Capt. C. T. O'Keefe 36th Inf. U.S.V.
224

John J. Pershing, Class of 1886, began his rise to prominence in the Philippines and became the American commander in chief in World War I.

Hugh L. Scott, Class of 1876, who made a reputation as a diplomat among the Western Indians, later served as superintendent of West Point (1906–1910) and Army chief of staff (1914–1917).

Tasker H. Bliss, Class of 1875, founded the Army War College and became Army chief of staff soon after America entered World War I.

Administration Of The New Empire

The real achievement of the West Point graduates in the Spanish-American War took place after the official peace, first in Cuba and later in the Philippines. Hugh Scott, Class of 1876, who had served as a diplomat among the Indians, and Tasker Bliss, Class of 1875, acted as chief of staff of the Department of Havana and collector of customs respectively under the military governor generalship of Leonard Wood. In four years this team working with such men as William Gorgas, who discovered the cause and antidote for yellow fever and who was the son of Josiah Gorgas, Class of 1841, chief of ordnance for the Confederate States, cleaned up what Scott called "a sickening mess." Thirteen times as many Americans had died in Cuba of disease as from battle wounds, and the chaos left behind by the moribund Spanish colonial government was everywhere. In addition to conquering the great tropical plague "yellow jack," the American occupation established the independence of Cuba.

In the Philippine Insurrection (as the guerrilla war that succeeded the Spanish withdrawal was known) and the American administration that followed, Hugh Scott again distinguished himself among the troublesome Moro tribes with military action and diplomatic negotiations similar to his work with the American Indians. Shortly before Scott went back to the United States to become superintendent of the Academy in 1906, his old friend Tasker Bliss arrived in the Philippines. Bliss had been engaged in establishing the War College, the graduate training school for young officers that would allow West Point to resume its functions of building character and revitalizing its academic standards. As Bliss returned to the War College in 1909, John J. Pershing, Class of 1886, who had begun his rise to prominence with his peformance as a captain in the 15th U.S. Cavalry against the Moros in 1902, became the military governor of Moro province. The careers of Scott, Bliss, and Pershing continued to interact through World War I.

Possession of the Philippines involved the United States in Far Eastern politics and the balance of European colonial power there. In 1900 the so-called "Boxer Rebellion" occurred, in which groups of fanatical Chinese attacked Europeans in China with the blessing of the government. The Boxer Rebellion called forth "relief expeditions" from the major European powers and the United States.

The Old Cadet Mess was replaced during the restoration of the campus by a building that could seat the entire Corps of Cadets together.

Change and Excitement At West Point

At the Academy itself, the excitement of these years was predictable after more than three decades during which the only combat a graduate could expect was on the bleak, dangerous, and inglorious frontier. Following the example of the Classes of 1861, the Class of 1898 demanded immediate graduation when war was declared, and within the week they were graduated (April 26) and sent to the war zone.

The new first class of 1899 was graduated in February 1899 to help combat the Philippine Insurrection, and in 1901 (after a year of normal graduation ceremonies) there was again a February graduation to release cadets for the Philippine Insurrection. As with previous, longer, and more complicated wars, however, the real relationship between the Academy and the war lay in the performance of older graduates such as Scott and Pershing, rather than in any immediate effect on West Point.

When the Old Academic Building was demolished in 1891, prior to the extensive renovation of the campus, one of the last traces of the classical, less bellicose architecture of West Point's early days disappeared. The Old Academic Building had been erected in 1838.

It may have been a certain resurgence of energy at West Point that the wars, expeditions, and insurrections implicitly provided, however, which caused the Association of Graduates, the War Department, and the national administration to look at West Point's physical plant. The centennial of the Academy was coming up in 1902 and the consensus after some examination was that the actual appearance and conditions of West Point's noble plateau were disgraceful. For the first time since Superintendent Delafield's Tudor building spree in the 1840s and 1850s there was an interest in an overall plan for West Point architecture.

In 1898, Cullum Memorial Hall, the first new building to be erected at West Point for decades, had been completed. Built with money left to the Academy by former Superintendent George Washington Cullum, the hall was dedicated to deceased officers and graduates of the military academy. It was built in a rather heavy Roman style with pillars

The headquarters of West Point's superintendent were photographed about 1900.

and few windows. Impressive as the building was, it was incongruous with the charming, rather provincial Victorian Tudor style of Superintendent Delafield's buildings, which seemed, with their soft gray stone, almost to grow up out of the Plain itself. Following the lead of the "Great White City" of exhibition buildings in Chicago at the World's Columbian Exposition of 1893, which had partly been designed by the prestigious New York City firm of McKim, Mead and White, a set of architecturally unified buildings was now thought to be desirable for exhibition spaces, government centers, and campuses. Accordingly, the War Department held a competition for architects to submit plans for completely revising the campus at West Point. In 1903 the contract went to the Boston firm of Cram, Goodhue and Ferguson, which had made a reputation by building in the Gothic Revival style popular in the middle of the 19th century. This style had been somewhat superseded by a taste for Neoclassical buildings such as Cullum Hall with pillars and domes and for the Beaux-Arts style in which the pillars and domes were embellished with such architectural refinements as cornices, carvings, and pediments. Ralph Adams Cram, however, the senior partner of Cram, Goodhue and Ferguson, had deep esthetic and philosophical beliefs about the vitality of Gothic architecture and, particularly, about its importance in relation to ritual such as the church and the Army practiced. This made his proposals

The Old Chapel (1836) first set the style of using local granite for Academy buildings. Classical Revival in style, it would be isolated among the more military English Tudor structures erected in the 1840s under Superintendent Delafield.

Before Edward S. Holden, Class of 1870, became Academy librarian in 1902, the old library shown here had few books other than out-of-date military histories.

for a Gothic West Point particularly appropriate, in addition to their being the perfect successor to the traditional Tudor style.

Congress had appropriated $6 million for the rebuilding of West Point, and between 1903 and 1913 the entire plant was rebuilt. The Post Headquarters, which was erected on the cliffs at the edge of the Plain, was related to the grand and rocky topography in the way of some medieval fortress or monastery on its mountain. When the chapel—designed by Cram's partner Bertram Goodhue—was completed in 1911 at the pinnacle of West Point's campus, the Academy's traditionally lofty aspirations were matched by its physical appearance.

Just before the post was reclothed in its new Gothic garb, Neoclassical Cullum Hall was the center of a sentimental but significant celebration. "June Week" 1902, the traditionally festive gradu-

ation week when government dignitaries, the Board of Visitors, military authorities, family, and ladies, ladies, ladies sailed up the river and climbed the road to the elm-draped Plain, was the official celebration of the Centennial of the United States Military Academy. President Theodore Roosevelt, Secretary of War Elihu Root (founder of the War College), and countless alumni and veterans assembled. When George Washington Cullum left money for his hall dedicated to the graduates, he had specified that no graduates who had served in the Confederate Army were to be commemorated. Consequently only Beauregard and Lee, in their capacities as superintendent, were mentioned. Times had changed, however, and the post Civil War attitude of Superintendent Cullum was no longer shared by many people connected with West Point, including veterans of the Civil War, North and South. The commissions of Rosser, Wheeler, and Lee in the Spanish-American War were vindicated on Alumni Day in 1902 when the chief speaker was General E. Porter Alexander, former chief of artillery in the Army of Northern Virginia. He affirmed the bravery of both sides in the Civil War and then expressed contentment with the ultimate results of the war. The band played the "Star-Spangled Banner" and then "Dixie," and dozens of elderly alumni embraced each other and wept. A wound that had been more physical than spiritual for West Point graduates was at last mended.

The new Cadet Chapel, completed in 1911, was the capstone of the extensive rebuilding of the campus designed by the Boston firm of Cram, Goodhue and Ferguson.

The Panama Canal

Concurrently with the affirmation of West Point as the ultimate military icon of a finally re-United States there came a vigorous demonstration of its old power and original purpose as the great source of engineering for the nation. Throughout most of the 19th century as American ships sailed from the East Coast to the newly acquired West Coast and as European ships sailed into the Pacific and on to the Orient, the trip around the southern tip of South America became more and more difficult and expensive. There had long been plans for a canal across the 40-mile wide Isthmus of Panama. In the late 19th century, the French, fresh from their

Under leadership of Col. George Washington Goethals, Class of 1880, the United States completed the Panama Canal in 1914. In order to clear land for the canal, some villages had to be evacuated and burned (below).

The 35,000 members of Colonel Goethals' work force used giant earth-moving machines to haul debris out of the canal cuts made-through the mountains.

triumph with the equally vital Suez Canal, undertook to dig a channel through Panama. The project was beset by problems with the heat; the wet soil, which kept falling back into excavations; and the deadly menace of yellow fever. The Americans took over in 1904 and beginning with the eradication of yellow fever directed by Colonel William Gorgas, who had triumphed over the disease in Cuba, American technology completed the canal.

Significantly, the historian Bruce Catton has said that "to mention this operation in the same breath . . . the Battle of Gettysburg is hardly to go out of line," and he goes on to quote President Theodore Roosevelt, one of the canal's great enthusiasts who said, "what is being done on the Isthmus [is] . . . one of the great feats of modern times . . . which can only be paralleled in our past history by some of the services rendered in certain wars." There, articulated once and for all, at a point vital to the growth of America, was the connection between the technology of warfare and the technology of growth. Naturally, the great engineer of the Panama Canal was a West Point man. Colonel George Washington Goethals, Class of 1880, son of Flemish immigrants from Brooklyn, had made a reputation as an engineer on the early Tennessee River damming and flood control projects before he was appointed chief

Colonel Goethals, shown reviewing Marines working on the Canal, was a determined commander who expected others to put in the same endless hours as he did.

engineer in Panama in 1907. John F. Stevens, an engineer who had planned the basic program of locks that would lift the canal from the Atlantic coast with its tide variation of less than a foot to the Pacific coast with its variation of more than 12 feet, worked for a time with Goethals and then resigned, although he retained Goethals's full respect. Goethals was an indefatigable worker who organized the engineering, labor, and lives of his 35,000 civilian workers. By working fourteen-hour days, driving his people hard but remaining accessible to hear their problems, and most importantly fully respecting Stevens's work, which coincided with his own engineering skills, Goethals accomplished be-

In the rocky mountainous sections, giant stone crushers helped the American engineers to overcome the constant problems presented by the terrain.

tween 1907 and 1914 what had been impossible during the previous thirty years.

Goethals's attitude admitted no defeat. When one of the last and most difficult sections, the Culebra Cut, was nearly obliterated by the mud of the Cucaracha slide in 1913, Goethals's answer to the questions of his subordinate, Lt. Col. David D. Gaillard (Class of 1884), about what to do was "Hell, dig it out again." The response may not have surprised Gaillard since the Cucaracha slide had dumped millions of tons of earth into the cut several times. When the canal was completed, Theodore Roosevelt, now no longer President but still regarding himself as the presiding genius of the canal, said, "Colonel Goethals has succeeded in instilling into the men under him a spirit which elsewhere has been found only in a few victorious armies." The brilliance of the founders of West Point in recognizing the connection between military organization and technology, on the one hand, and great civil works on the other, was as plain as the band of water connecting the oceans.

The Punitive Expedition into Mexico in 1916 followed raids by Pancho Villa on U.S. towns. In a forecast of World War I, Company A, 6th Infantry, packed the trench protecting its camp.

The Mexican Border Campaign

As the opening of the canal in 1914 confirmed in part the worth of the Academy's original engineering aims, so an earlier conflict was nearly revived in the years after the Centennial in the troubles on the Mexican border. The Mexican War of 1846–1848 had been primarily a way for the United States to claim land that Americans had already begun to settle. The boundaries established in 1848 had held good for more than half a century when trouble broke out in 1916. Mexico had been governed firmly but despotically in the later 19th century by Porfirio Diaz, a white-mustachioed old patrician who stabilized the government after the chaos of the French intervention of the 1860s but worsened, if possible, the poverty and servitude of the Mexican poor.

In 1910 a number of rebellions broke out against Diaz, eruptions that assumed the proportions of a full-scale revolution. There were a number of independently operating warlords who raided the nearby United States, leading to a concentration of Army units along the border and eventual American

Pursuing Villa, Battery C, 6th Field Artillery, rests near Dolores, Mexico, in 1916. Artillery transport had changed little since the Napoleonic Wars.

support of Venustiano Carranza, a main claimant of the presidency of Mexico. Francisco Villa, known as "Pancho," was the illiterate, buccaneering guerrilla chief of the northern states that abutted on Texas, New Mexico, and Arizona. Although Villa was once a Carranza supporter, Villa's band had killed a number of Americans, frequently business travelers, in Mexico. These actions had gone a long way toward arousing American ire before he plundered Nogales, Arizona, in 1915 and then in March 1916 attacked Columbus, New Mexico, in a devastating raid that resulted in the deaths of sixteen Americans.

General Hugh L. Scott, who had left his post as superintendent of the military academy to become Army chief of staff, and his assistant, Major General Tasker Bliss, had recommended their colleague from the Philippine campaigns, Brigadier General John J. Pershing, to lead the forces against Mexico instead of the man on the spot, General Frederick Funston. Pershing, who had risen swiftly since the Philippine days (in 1906, President Roo-

sevelt had promoted him to brigadier general over 862 senior officers), was waiting on the border with 6,000 troops for the order to march.

In April 1916, Pershing and his men began the Punitive Expedition, a march that would take them 300 miles into the Mexican interior. There were eight cavalry regiments, five artillery batteries, and five infantry regiments, plus ordnance, signal, quartermaster, ambulance, and engineer detachments. The territory through which they marched was alternately impenetrable granite mountains and desert in which the temperature would shift forty or fifty degrees between daylight and nighttime. The native people, although they welcomed Yankee money and were not hostile, were both sympathetic to and terrified of Pancho Villa. They would tell the Americans that they had seen him a few hours before when he was miles away or that he had been killed when he was in fact about to attack. Finally the official Mexican federal government began to be nervous about so large a troop of American soldiers within its borders and began to hamper the efforts

Handwritten on photo: Preparing mess In camp at Ft. Sam Houston,

Maneuvers at Fort Sam Houston, in San Antonio, Texas, prepared the Army for the Mexican border campaign and, ultimately, World War I.

Brigadier General Pershing (left) leads his men across a river in 1916 during the Punitive Expedition.

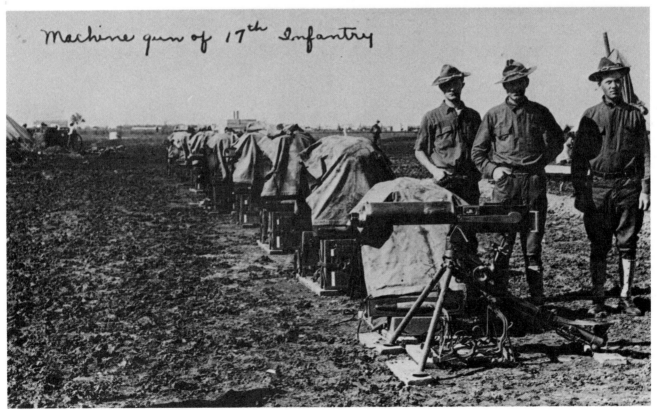

Handwritten on photo: Machine gun of 17th Infantry

173

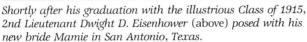

Shortly after his graduation with the illustrious Class of 1915, 2nd Lieutenant Dwight D. Eisenhower (above) posed with his new bride Mamie in San Antonio, Texas.

Lieutenant George S. Patton (above right) looks both dapper and belligerent while serving in the Mexican border campaign as Pershing's aide-de-camp.

Brigadier General Pershing (far right) wrote letters near Casas Grandes, Mexico, on March 26, 1916.

of the expedition. At last the Mexican government and President Wilson agreed to withdraw the troops. As General Pershing himself wrote in his memoirs, "the increasing disapproval of the Mexican Government doubtless caused the administration to conclude . . . that the people of northern Mexico had been taught a salutary lesson . . ."

When the American troops withdrew in February 1917, Villa had not been captured and few battles had been waged; on the other hand the United States had lost few men, they had asserted the nation's right to defend with maximum force any attack on its borders, and about a thousand fledgling U.S. officers had been given experience in the field that would be useful in a grim way very soon on the battlefields of France.

Life At The Academy

The Mexican Border Campaign brought to an end what hindsight could see to be the last of the "little wars," the preparatory wars for what would popularly be called "the great conflagration over there." In World War I, which was unique in American history up to that point in that America's involvement in it was an acknowledgment that the United States had become a world power, West Point would lead as it had in all other American conflicts. Of the thirty-eight American corps and division commanders in France during 1917 and 1918, thirty-four were West Point graduates. They had come, however, from a school that was continuing the tradition that had settled in after the Civil War—a tradition of conservative academic training and strong emphasis on character. General Henry H. Arnold, a graduate of 1907, remembered that "we lived . . . in conformance with a code, and with daily routines which had not changed strikingly . . . since Grant was a cadet."

Between the Centennial celebration of 1902 and the beginning of World War I for America in 1917, there had been some rather glacially slow progress in the modernization of the Academy. The rebuilding program engaged in between 1903 and 1913 extensively changed the appearance of the Point, or at least spruced it up dramatically; and there were some rather important curriculum changes in the tactical department under the direction of Commandant Otto T. Hein, Class of 1870. Commandant Hein ameliorated the genteel distance between the life of a cadet, where the rigor was gymnastic and any contact with the outside world took place during

In the aftermath of the Spanish-American War, West Point attracted fashionable visitors who were treated to displays like this Gatling gun demonstration.

the gentility of summer camp, and the life of a soldier in combat. On cross-country marches Hein required cadets, for the first time, to carry their own gear and set up camp themselves, instead of bringing enlisted men along to do the heavy work. He also initiated a program of instruction in the use of the Gatling gun, the mortar battery, and other implements of modern warfare. Finally, Hein saw to it that command duty in camp was rotated so that cadets learned the duties of different ranks, and during the academic year he gave a course on the practical administrative duties of an officer, such as recruiting, making reports, and serving as quartermaster.

During the years between the Centennial and 1917, West Point accelerated its long-standing program of physical exercise and gymnastics. Colonel Herman Koehler gave a complete course in calisthenics that fourth class cadets were required to take and upper classmen could if they wanted to; and instruction in advanced riding, fencing, boxing, wrestling, and swimming were offered as well.

When Hugh L. Scott became superintendent in 1906 between his tours of duty in the Philippines and his service as Army chief of staff, he was the first superintendent since Thayer to realize that West Point's image as a symbol of national virtue and might could be enhanced by an active public relations campaign. The newspapers had been cool about the Academy since the death of Cadet Booz, whether from his enforced hazing and drinking of tabasco sauce or not, and Superintendent Scott worked to reverse the Academy's forbidding image as a stronghold of conservatism and military brutality. He courted reporters, invited the public to visit, and built rest rooms and drinking fountains. Soon one of the most popular stops on the Hudson River Day Line excursion boat trips was the South Dock at West Point. During these year Frances Benjamin Johnston, photographer and chronicler of the American scene who had photographed the residents of the White House, Tuskegee Institute, and the icy-crisp, white-clad officers of Admiral Dewey's Great White Fleet when it steamed back from Manila, came up to West Point and took some of the most sensitive images the camera had ever recorded there.

The Class of 1915—known as the "Class the Stars Fell On" because 59 of its 164 graduates reached the rank of brigadier general or above—visited the Gettysburg battlefield just before graduation.

The Old Guard And The Young Lions

Still, despite these relatively minor adjustments to the 20th century, the Academy changed little. The Old Guard graduates with their sentimental investment in the past and the Academic Board with its vested interests in the status quo were vocal in their desire to maintain what they saw as perfection. It was in 1917 that an alumnus wrote: "The great charm of West Point is that so many things never change." The almost inexplicable irony is that however archaic and inappropriate for modern warfare the West Point curriculum was, the conservatives seemed to be proven right by the fact that whenever West Point graduates were put to the test, they were intrepid, imaginative, and intelligent. Scott, Bliss, Goethals, and Pershing had all come out of the doldrum years after the Civil War. Douglas MacArthur, one of the greatest generals the world has ever known, and one who would have a direct and revolutionary influence on West Point, was a product of those years, and in 1915 came "the class the stars fell on." Among its 164 graduates, 59 attained the rank of brigadier general or higher. The entire course of the world in the middle of the 20th century would be determined by these men. The mold from which they came, the source of their strength, was the United States Military Academy.

Dwight D. Eisenhower (above), Bradley's classmate, also reached five-star rank and was elected President.

Omar Bradley (left), one of the two five-star generals the Class of 1915 produced, distinguished himself as a cadet on the baseball field.

Omar N. Bradley, victor in Africa and Normandy during World War II, Chief of Staff of the Army during the Korean War; James A. Van Fleet, Commanding General of the Eighth Army in Korea; and Dwight D. Eisenhower, Supreme Commander, Allied Forces in Europe, during World War II and President of the United States, were three of the best-known graduates of the remarkable Class of 1915. George S. Patton, a brilliant and erratic graduate of the Class of 1909, would work closely, usually productively, and sometimes infuriatingly, with many of the 1915 graduates during World War II. The differences in personality between Patton on the one hand and officers like Bradley and Eisen-

George S. Patton, noted as a cadet for his aristocratic flamboyance, was as outstanding in personality during his cadet years as he would be later in World War II.

hower on the other illustrated the flexibility that West Point training allowed, rigid as it sometimes seemed.

Patton, known as "Georgie" to his classmates, was an aristocrat who dressed and lived flamboyantly and who gave in with sometimes disastrous self-indulgence to an almost ungovernable temper. During World War II his genius for leading men and for prosecuting difficult campaigns in Sicily in 1943 and Germany in 1944 was tarnished by a much-publicized incident in which he slapped a soldier who had been relieved of duty for battle fatigue. One positive effect of Patton's flamboyance was his charismatic leadership of his men, who gained self-respect and a sense of distinction from his high standards of dress and drill. The entry in the 1909 *Howitzer* yearbook for Patton, after noting his nickname "Georgie" and listing his athletic achievements, has a paragraph of fantasy that any Third Army GI thirty-five years later would immediately recognize:

> *Confusion reigned supreme. The barracks were being shaken by a violent earthquake, and men came tumbling out of their divisions in all stages of dishabilie. Suddenly . . . Cadet Lieutenant and Adjutant [Patton] appeared in the area, faultlessly attired, as usual. Walking with a firm step across the area, he halted, executed a proper about face, and the stentorian tones rang out, 'Battalion Attention-n-n-n! Cadets will refrain from being unduly shaken up. There will be no yelling in the area. The earthquake will cease immediately!'*

Patton's field experience began in the Mexican border campaign with General Pershing. In World War I, Patton served with distinction and showed great foresight with his interest in the possibilities of tanks and armored warfare. As with many other American leaders, Patton's World War I services laid the groundwork for his forceful leadership and tactical brilliance in World War II, when he worked with his old friend and former subordinate, Dwight D. Eisenhower. It is marvelous, in looking back at the careers of men like Patton and the many generals of the Class of 1915, to realize that while they capably directed millions of soldiers in wars lasting years, in earlier eras they might well have spent their military lives in administrative duties and colonial skirmishes as hundreds of their predecessors had.

While "Georgie" Patton had been noted for flamboyance, Omar Bradley and Dwight Eisenhower were fulfilling the roles of model cadets, rather than class characters. Bradley was a schoolmaster's son from Clark, Missouri, who during his years as a cadet established a reputation for deceptively slow, sure skill on the baseball field where he would lope toward a fly ball with maddeningly unhurried certainty, catch it, and then, with what was called the finest throwing arm in Army history, toss it where it would do the most damage. Dwight Eisenhower, the son of a poor family from Abilene, Kansas, had worked nights in a creamery to help his family while he was still in high school and had applied for admission to either of the service academies, Annapolis or West Point, as a way of getting out of Abilene. At the Academy he was a halfback on the football team until he hurt his knee in the middle of the 1912 season, and then he was a cheerleader for the rest of his time as a cadet.

The Mystique of West Point

A sense of what the Academy meant to these men, beyond a means of escape from poverty or tedium in pre-World War I small towns, beyond a career with some hope of excitement or involvement in national affairs, was suggested later by General Eisenhower in talking about the West Point honor system. When Eisenhower was chief of staff after World War II and was working on a revision of the Academy curriculum with Superintendent Maxwell Taylor he asserted that "the one thing that has set West Point definitely apart from every other school in the world is the fact that for a number of years it has not only had an 'honor' system but that the system has actually worked." He went on to compare a graduate's feeling about the honor system to his feeling about his mother.

The honor system, which was not formally codified until after Eisenhower's graduation, had nonetheless been part of the West Point system of self-policing since the 1870s, when cadets monitored the honesty of their peers with a self-appointed Vigilance Committee. Sylvanus Thayer's code of gentlemanly behavior carried explicitly and implicitly the injunction that a man's word was his bond. A gentleman did not lie under any circumstances, and if he did he must be drummed out of the company of gentlemen. Pranks that went against Academy rules were part of a time-honored tradition, from the days of Jefferson Davis breaking his leg returning from an off-limits visit to Benny Havens to Eisenhower making clandestine trips to Newburgh with fellow cadets for late night snacks. However, if challenged, cadets were expected to tell the truth to superiors and peers at all times.

Eisenhower's suggestion of a deep emotional response to a tradition that represents a standard of behavior perhaps explains the mystique of West Point. It explains the feeling on the part of cadets and graduates that they had come through an initiation that forever marked them for a special destiny. This sense, inculcated into the Class of 1915 and other pre-World War I classes, was to bloom in full and awful power under the pressure of war, but the dramatic performance in combat would not have been possible without the sense of having undergone a unique intellectual, physical, and spiritual preparation. Just as medieval knights prepared for their calling with years of serving an older knight climaxed by a night-long vigil of prayer, so West Point cadets had gone through a particular ritualistic four-year apprenticeship to graduate with a complete sense of commitment.

A Military Family: A Portfolio

West Point's tradition of service to the nation often passed from generation to generation in the same families. Some families were nationally known, but most were typical Americans who developed a military tradition, often strengthened through marriage with other West Point families. The Bennets began their association with the Academy during the Indian Wars and extended their service well into the 20th century. The first two generations fought from the Philippine Insurrection through World War II.

John Bradbury Bennet, Class of 1891, married Nellie Dent Sharp, a niece of U.S. Grant. Two of the Bennets' sons (below) graduated from West Point.

John Bennington Bennet, Class of 1916, taught at West Point and served in both world wars. His son graduated from the Academy, and his daughter married a West Pointer.

Alexander Sharp Bennet, Class of 1919, an artilleryman, fought in both the China and Pacific theaters in World War II.

Captain Bennet (above) poses about 1905 with his sons (from left) John, Hiram, and Alexander while stationed in California after his first tour in the Philippines.

Brigadier General Bennet (above, second from left) *receives the French Legion of Merit at Le Havre in 1919.*

Alexander Bennet stands formally (top right) *for a graduation photograph with his mother.*

(Top left) *With his wife, Nellie, whose two sisters married West Pointers, Bennet returned to the Philippines as inspector general of the constabulary, 1907–1911.*

In Washington after World War I Brigadier General Bennet joined the personnel section of the War Department's general staff.

American soldiers, part of the large, unified U.S. force, advance towards the front in the Marne offensive of 1918.

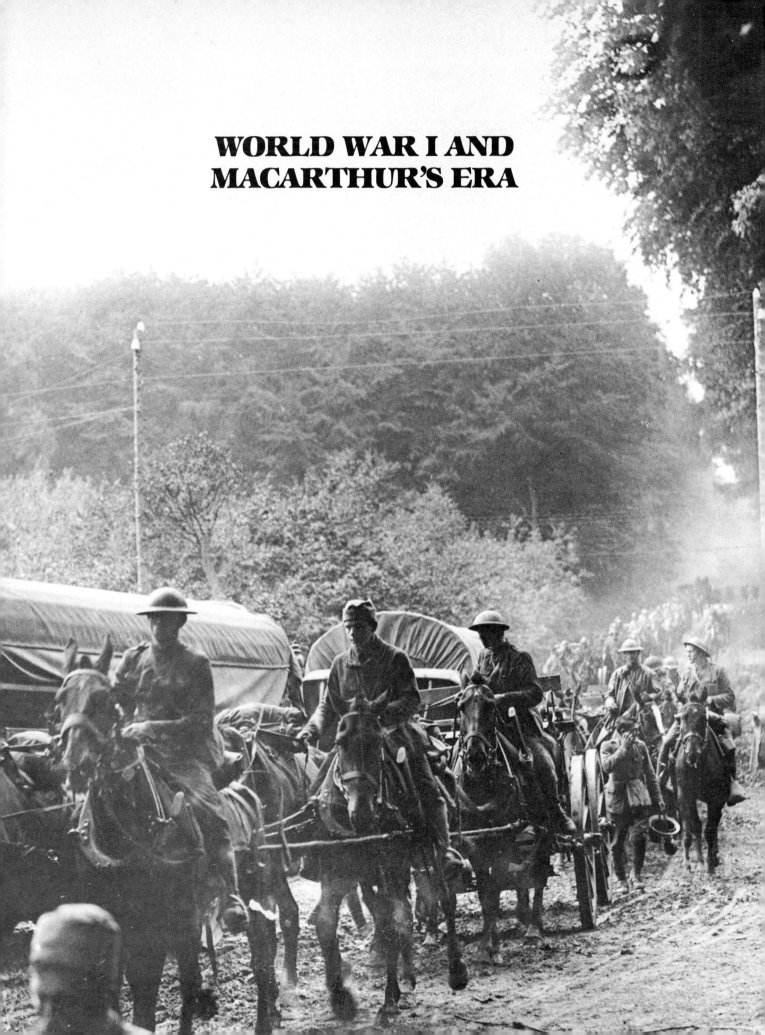

WORLD WAR I AND MACARTHUR'S ERA

When the United States actually entered World War I on April 6, 1917, there had been nearly three years of war in Europe and three years of agonizing on the part of many Americans, particularly by President Woodrow Wilson. Originally determined to stay out of what was regarded popularly as a dynastic conflict between the decadent old powers of Europe, America was gradually drawn in by German attacks on vessels carrying American citizens (such as the sinking of the *Lusitania* in 1915, with the loss of 128 American lives); by the realization, despite clandestine diplomatic missions to London, Paris, and Berlin, that it would be impossible to mediate or settle the war any way other than militarily; and by the vision of what "peace without victory" would mean not only for Europe but also for America. When in early 1917 the British decoded and sent to President Wilson the so-called "Zimmerman Note," war was inevitable. In the note (actually a cabled message) the German minister of foreign affairs instructed Germany's Mexican ambassador to offer Mexico the states of Arizona, New Mexico, and Texas if Mexico entered the conflict on the German side if the United States went to war against Germany. Germany's potential ally would be led by Venustiano Carranza, who had vacillated in dealing with the Americans during the Mexican Border Campaign. The further discovery that Germany had spent $27 million for espionage in the United States in 1915 alone made war the only alternative. President Wilson declared to a joint session of Congress that:

> *It is a fearful thing to lead this great peaceful people into war, into the most terrible and disastrous of all wars, civilization itself seeming to be in the balance. But the right is more precious than peace, and we shall fight for the things which we have always carried nearest our hearts ...*

Sitting on a motorcycle with a sidecar, an officer with his men watches a biplane at the U.S. Army School of Aerial Photography in Ithaca, N.Y.

During one of the periodic attempts in the pre-World War I years to modernize the training program at West Point, an "automobile wireless"—a car to which messages could be telegraphed—was one of the more bizarre experiments.

The fact that West Point men would lead America in the World War as they had in every other war was evident, even evident to the point of commissioned civilians complaining about the fraternal preference West Point men gave each other in promotions and decision making, just as the volunteers had complained about the Regular Army during the Civil War. Just how the West Pointers would lead the Army and how that army would fit into the three-year-old entrenched campaigns of the French and English, however, were determined by West Point men also. Hugh L. Scott, that unsung genius of American military history, was chief of staff, but in 1917 he had been sent on a negotiating mission

to the Kerensky government in Russia, leaving his long-time colleague Tasker Bliss in Washington as acting chief of staff. Bliss, with his vast experience from the Indian days with Scott through the Philippine campaigns and the administration of the War College, understood international military diplomacy as well as anyone in power. With the cooperation of Secretary of War Newton Baker, who trusted the advice of his professional military associates, and with the appointment of John J. Pershing, Bliss's long-time confederate from the Philippine days, as commander, the American Expeditionary Force was launched with a complete understanding of its duties and hazards.

Wearing the distinctive "doughboy" uniform characteristic of World War I, enlisted men training in the United States for the war in Europe line up at the mess hall.

Letter writing in the trenches of France was less civilized than this photograph in a training tent suggests. Censorship in World War I led to such letterhead notations as "Somewhere in France."

The American Role

The French, English, and Italians, after three years of bloodletting on a scale never before known in the history of warfare, desperately needed American help. However, as Acting Chief of Staff Tasker Bliss concisely put it in a memo to Secretary of War Baker on May 25, 1917, "What the English and French really wanted from us was not a large, well-trained army but a large number of smaller units which they could feed promptly into their lines as parts of their own organizations."

President Wilson, made aware of the danger that his army would be fragmented and used without proper respect for its autonomy and voluntary entry into the war, gave General Pershing one official directive that simply assumed that the American Expeditionary Force would function independently of the French and the English and a second, private one that said: "You are directed to cooperate with the forces of the other countries employed against [the] enemy; but in so doing the underlying idea must be kept in view that the forces of the United States are a separate and distinct component . . . the identity of which must be preserved."

Through much of 1917, Pershing resisted the attempts of the Supreme Allied War Council to fragment American forces. France's Marshal Ferdinand Foch, Supreme Allied Commander, had numerous confrontations with Pershing, who was supported by French General Henri Philippe Pétain and President Wilson. But by 1918 conscription had been instituted for the first time since the Civil War, and nearly 4 million Americans were available to fight. In the two German offensives of 1918, Pershing did indeed allow these Americans to be directed by Foch. It has been thought that if the Germans had not activated the offensives of 1918 the war could have dragged on almost indefinitely. Contemporary weapons and explosives had become so effective that soldiers charging a trench had almost no chance of victory and casualties were enormous. With the stalemate of the trenches, however, keeping both sides from victory, the Germans (who had contributed to Russia's withdrawal from the war by aiding revolutionaries in the Rusian Revolution) decided to concentrate on an active offensive in March. After the first of five annihilating offensives by the Germans, Pershing came to Foch with the statement: "I have come to tell you that the American people would consider it a great honor for our troops to be engaged in the present battle. . . ."

In July 1918, Pershing, Foch, and the British commanders—backed up by the French and British governments—requested more American troops to stop the Germans, who had once again reached the Marne, within shelling distance of Paris, just as they had in 1914. On July 15 the last German offensive, known as the Second Battle of the Marne, was launched. The German commander later wrote:

Pershing (right) *confers in France with Maj. Gen. Charles D. Rhodes, Class of 1889, and Charles G. Dawes* (back to camera), *then helping to supervise military supply operations and later U.S. vice president.*

In March 1919, having resisted English and French efforts to disperse American units within their commands, General Pershing and Maj. Gen. Joseph Dickman (Class of 1881) proudly posed at Valendar, Germany, with the massed men and officers of the 2nd Division.

"We well-nigh reached the objectives prescribed for with the exception of the one division on our right wing. This encountered American units." Foch called upon the U.S. 1st and 2nd Divisions, a French division, and an English one to make a counterattack at Soissons. This, wrote General Pershing, "turned the tide of war." The German chancellor, who was expecting a surrender from the Allies on the 15th, knew on the 18th "that all was lost. The history of the world was played out in three days."

With continued Allied offensives, including the participation of a now fully recognized American army, the German line was broken. The Argonne battle, launched on September 26, was the greatest in which American troops—896,000 of them—had ever fought. On November 11 the Armistice was signed.

The thirty-four out of thirty-eight American division and corps commanders in the war who were West Point men again proved the incredible, almost mystical efficiency of the Academy's training. Secretary of War Baker, who had placed such trust in Pershing and Tasker Bliss, said in 1919: "West Point again demonstrated its supreme value to the country in the hour of need. In all walks of life character is the indispensable basis of enduring

Alfred M. Gruenther, Class of 1919, like many West Pointers, just missed service in World War I but reached high command in World War II.

success. West Point does many things for its men, but the highest quality it gives them is character, and in the emergency of the World War, our success rested on the character of our leaders." He almost exactly paralleled the tribute General Winfield Scott had paid to West Point after the Mexican War.

Status of the Academy

And yet, ironically, just as the value of West Point was again proven, its rusty internal mechanism—which had been virtually dismantled by the emergency need for officers—was finally recognized as being almost inoperable. As had happened in 1861 and all through the Spanish-American War and the Philippine Insurrection, the cadets who were at the Academy when the war began graduated after shorter courses of instruction. The Class of 1917

graduated in April 1917, soon after the declaration of war, while the Class of 1918 graduated in August 1917. The Class of 1919 graduated in 1918 and on November 1, 1918, the classes of 1920 and 1921 graduated, leaving only one class at the post. When the war was over, the November graduates returned to the post for an additional six months' instruction, but because they were commissioned officers they had an ambiguous status as cadets. A new class was also admitted in November 1918, but because there was only one regular class at the Academy, the new class could not be treated as plebes, so they too had an ambiguous status, somewhere between cadet and veteran. The new superintendent who arrived in June 1919 and who would be perhaps the best known officer to have occupied that post since Robert E. Lee made the observation that "the entire institution [is] in a state of disorder and confusion." Brigadier General Douglas MacArthur vowed to do something about that.

MacArthur, Class of 1903, who had undergone extraordinary hazing because he was the son of General Arthur MacArthur, hero of the Philippines, knew the best and the worst of the Academy. Arthur MacArthur, a Medal of Honor winner in the Civil War, had also been a commander of Pershing, under whom Douglas served. The links between Pershing and Douglas MacArthur were further strengthened by the fact that each had been first captain of his class at West Point. This West Point bond showed at the front in World War I when Pershing remarked to MacArthur, "We old first captains, Douglas, must never flinch." MacArthur's own ego and skill had aided his meteoric rise during World War I when he had helped to generate public acceptance of conscription and when he then served as chief of staff of the 42nd Division, the Rainbow Division, in France.

General Pershing reviews the cadets at gradution in 1920, followed by Superintendent MacArthur and other dignitaries.

When he was appointed superintendent of the military academy by Chief of Staff Peyton March, Class of 1888, March hoped that MacArthur would take the opportunity of the chaos in the Academy's structure caused by the war to deal with its basic lack of relevance to the modern world. Although the Academy obviously could not be called a failure in any way with the continued, conspicuous success of its graduates, the lack of communication between West Point graduates and the volunteers and draftees of a citizens' army, the single biggest problem and one that had dogged it since the Civil War, was now all the more marked. In an age of technological warfare, with tanks and explosives decimating whole divisions, when officers had to be trained as experts in minute areas of scientific warfare, West Point's old boast of leading with character was simply not sufficient. The methods of fighting in World War I, which involved the concepts of total war implemented by Sherman in the Civil War—with technological advances unimagined before—engaged whole populations—civilian and military—and the sky as well as the sea and the land. No traditional study of tactics, augmented by character

building and cavalry expertise would be effective in this new world. MacArthur, surveying the West Point curriculum, asked with his customary dramatic effect, "How long are we going to go on preparing for the War of 1812?"

Superintendent MacArthur

Although MacArthur did implement some classroom and curriculum changes while he was at West Point (and did so over the vehement protests of the Academic Board, many of whom had been professors when he was a cadet), his greatest contribution was to open West Point to the world and engage the Academy and the cadets with the citizens and circumstances that they would have to encounter professionally and personally. The notion of the Academy as a military cloister breeding knights errant was not useful in the 20th century. *The New York Times* asserted in 1919 that "We need less 'pipeclay' and less seclusion at the Military Academy—in one word, more democracy." Superintendent MacArthur agreed. He attempted to broaden the faculty's outlook by sending each faculty member to another academic institution of his choosing

Under Superintendent MacArthur after World War I summer camp became more realistic but the cadet yearbook still recorded frivolous moments such as a "foraging expedition" to a watermelon patch (left) *and washing up* (above) *at Monroe, New York.*

for one month per year; he had cadets read daily newspapers in English class; and, in an attempt to stiffen up the cadets and make their field training more realistic, he continued the reforms of Commandant Hein from earlier in the century and replaced the rather frivolous summer camp with a program of basic training at New Jersey's Fort Dix— to and from which the cadets had to march. He also replaced the study of Civil War battlefields (an innovation amazingly of the early 20th century) with studies of the battlefields of France in the recent war. To the consternation of the alumni and the faculty alike, he further broke down West Point's seclusion by allowing the cadets reasonable pay, free time to go off the post, and, on summer weekends, overnight passes so that they could go to New York City. Like Sylvanus Thayer, whom he in some ways resembled, MacArthur's concerns were with big issues. He was reasonable with his superiors, such as

In 1919 the incoming plebes (left) *appeared more military than their earlier counterparts, and upperclassmen herded them smartly through their first days* (below left). *As superintendent, MacArthur maintained some traditions, such as appearance* (below), *and called for sweeping changes in other areas.*

A summer encampment after World War I uses the same Indian-style tents of the Civil War era, while cadets train for 20th century warfare.

Brig. Gen. Douglas MacArthur, with a brilliant combat record in World War I, implemented sweeping changes while West Point's superintendent from 1919 to 1922. *(right)*

members of the War Department, and strict but fair with cadets, sometimes turning a gentlemanly blind eye to minor infractions of the rules when he encountered cadets in places where they ought not to be. However, with his immediate subordinates, such as the Academic Board, he was autocratic and did not bother to explain the logic behind his drastic reforms.

Two of his reforms that were aimed at codifying the issue of character building and taking it out of the nebulous area of "gentlemanly behavior" were a systematization of the Honor Code (administration of the code by the cadets was formalized) and a figuring of all points of conduct into the weekly class ranking system. MacArthur was a great believer in the benefits—physical and mental—of exercise and athletics. He increased the emphasis on athletics and to show how important he considered their role at the Academy had these lines carved into the stone at the entrance to the gym:

Upon the fields of friendly strife
Are sown the seeds
That, upon other fields, on other days
Will bear the fruits of victory

In January 1922, Chief of Staff John J. Pershing, perhaps as a result of the widespread dissatisfaction with MacArthur's extreme reforms, announced that he was posting him to the Philippines as of June so that instead of the customary four-year tour as superintendent, MacArthur had little more than three. With his departure, inevitably, many of his reforms were reversed and it seemed that the 20th century and the concept of total warfare that involved citizen armies led by trained specialists had only blown through West Point and moved on. But this was not so; once the reforms had been considered many of them were kept in mind.

MacArthur foresaw the future role of West Point when he suggested, shortly before leaving for the Philippines, that the Corps of Cadets be increased in size. In the report he wrote:

By superior organization, system and efficiency, West Point can turn out annually for its country's service twice the number of qualified men it is now graduating. With the peacetime demand for trained officers, the number of officers is certain to fall far short

of requirements. And if this condition holds in time of peace how much greater will be the insufficiency in time of national emergency. West Point has been reconstructed upon the same ideals of public service which it has held from its inception. Its graduates will be a bulwark to the nation in the future as they have been in the past. I can but hope that the dictates of wisdom will prevail and that their number will be steadily increased to correspond with the urgent needs of our country in peace or in war.

West Point was too valuable and too integral a part of the American spirit for it to be ignored. Generals Pershing, Scott, March, and Bliss had won a war because they were officers and gentlemen. Eisenhower, Patton, Bradley, and Van Fleet, and many others would win their stars and their country's glory because they were West Point men. But the world to come was very different from the world these men had known. It took World War I to suggest how total a holocaust the 20th century would yet know, and if the ideals and intelligence of West Point were to work in that world, the Academy would have to adapt. MacArthur had shown the way. In the years following his superintendency life on the Plain above the river would meet the life of the world from which West Point could no longer isolate itself.

CHRONOLOGY

The history of West Point has both paralleled and developed separately from that of the United States. Significant events at the Academy sometimes related directly to events in the nation, particularly during war, and at other times occurred without apparent reference to the larger stage. Below is a brief summary of the high points of West Point history and of U.S. political, diplomatic, and military events that influenced the military academy and its graduates.

West Point

1802 Congress authorizes President Thomas Jefferson to organize a military academy at West Point: March 16.

Jonathan Williams becomes 1st superintendent: April 15.

Academy formally opened at West Point: July 4.

First graduation examinations: September 1.

United States Military Philosophical Society formed, modeled on Britain's Royal Society: November 12.

1805 Jonathan Williams, who had left in June 1803, returns to become 2nd superintendent: April 19.

1808 Congress authorizes expansion of Corps of Cadets to 156: April 12.

1812 Congress authorizes increased academic staff and expansion of Corps of Cadets to 250; entrance requirements specified: April 29.

Joseph G. Swift becomes 3rd superintendent: July 31.

1814 Capt. Alexander J. Williams becomes only West Pointer to die in combat in War of 1812, at Fort

United States

1802 Judiciary Act sets number of Supreme Court justices at six, with each also, heading a circuit court: April 29.

1803 Territory known as Louisiana Purchase bought from France: April 30.

Lewis and Clark Expedition begins exploration of Far West: August 31.

1804 Thomas Jefferson reelected President: December.

1807 Embargo Act restricts foreign commerce; U.S.-British economic and political actions increase tensions between two countries; 1807–1811.

New York City-Albany roundtrip by Robert Fulton's *Clermont* starts age of steam: August.

1808 James Madison elected President: December.

1811 Gen. William Henry Harrison's forces defeat Indians under Tecumseh at Tippecanoe: November 7–8.

1812 War of 1812 begins as United States declares war on Britain: June 19.

James Madison reelected President: December.

1813 U.S. victory in Battle of Lake Erie enables Americans to regain initiative after series of defeats: September 10.

William Henry Harrison's troops defeat British at Battle of Thames: October 5.

1814 British forces burn Washington, D.C.: August 24–25.

West Point

Erie: August 15.

1815 Duties of superintendent of West Point and of Army's chief engineer separated.

Alden Partridge becomes 4th superintendent: January 3.

1816 Benny Havens establishes his famous tavern in Highland Falls.

Board of Visitors established.

Sec. of War William Crawford issues rules setting general examinations of cadets; four-year course of study specified: March.

Amosophic Society, Academy's first literary group, established: May 4.

Color of cadet uniform changed from blue to gray, to honor Winfield Scott's gray-clad troops at Battle of Chippewa: September 4.

1817 Sylvanus Thayer becomes 5th superintendent: July 28.

Thayer establishes Lt. George W. Gardiner in assignment later known as Commandant of Cadets: September 15.

1818 Congress authorizes a Chaplain for the Academy: April 14.

Group of cadets, favoring former Superintendent Partridge, presents grievances but is rebuffed by Superintendent Thayer: November.

Cadets held to be subject to military law: November.

1819 First summer camp held just west of Fort Clinton.

1820 Cadet Corps marches to Philadelphia; summer expeditions inaugurated by Superintendent Thayer brought Academy recognition and favorable publicity.

Superintendent's quarters completed.

1821 Cadet Corps' summer march is to Boston. Congressional motion to abolish the Academy, although unsuccessful, showed divided opinions on value of West Point: February 16.

United States

1815 Gen. Andrew Jackson, unaware of peace signed December 24, 1814, defeats British at Battle of New Orleans: January 8.

Congress sets peacetime Army at 10,000: March 3.

1816 James Monroe elected President: December.

1819 Under Adams-Onis Treaty Florida goes to United States, which gives up claim to Texas: February 22.

1820 Missouri Compromise attempts to balance number of free and slave states: March 3.

James Monroe reelected President: December.

1823 Monroe Doctrine defines U.S. policy in the West-

West Point

1824 The Dialectic Society, a literary and debating organization, established.

1828 Kosciusko Monument given to Academy by Corps of Cadets; designed by John H. Latrobe, a Class of 1822 non-graduate.

1829 West Point Hotel built at west edge of the plain.

1830 Dennis Hart Mahan joins faculty.

1833 Colonel Thayer relieved of duty as superintendent at his own request: July 1.

Rene E. DeRussy becomes 6th superintendent: July 1.

1834 Report by Committee on Military Affairs to Congress notes great civil engineering contributions of Academy graduates: March 17.

1835 First class rings made for Class of 1835.

1837 Old Chapel designed in Classical Revival style.

Professor Dennis Hart Mahan publishes his renowned *Elementary Course of Civil Engineering.*

1838 Congress requires graduates to serve for four

United States

ern Hemisphere: December 2.

1825 John Quincy Adams elected President by House of Representatives as no candidate had electoral majority in 1824 election: February 9.

Erie Canal opens; begins canal boom: October.

1826 Mohawk and Hudson Railroad chartered; U.S. rail network grows rapidly until Civil War.

1828 Andrew Jackson elected President: December.

1831 Slave rebellion led by Nat Turner: August.

1832 Andrew Jackson reelected President: December.

1836 Samuel Colt patents his revolver in United States.

Texas secedes from Mexico; Mexican troops massacre Americans in Alamo (March 6); Texans victorious at decisive Battle of San Jacinto (April 21).

Martin Van Buren elected President: December.

years: July 5.

Richard Delafield becomes 7th superintendent: September 1.

1839 Training in horsemanship begins.

1840 William Henry Harrison elected President: December.

1841 Library, in English Tudor style, completed.

1841 President Harrison dies; succeeded by Vice President John Tyler: April 4.

1842 President Tyler authorizes use of federal troops, if necessary, in Rhode Island's Dorr Rebellion.

1843 Congress provides that one cadet can be appointed from each Congressional district and that the President can appoint ten cadets "at large": March 1.

1844 James K. Polk elected President: December.

1845 New barracks construction, in English Tudor style, started.

1845 Annexation of Texas (March 1) increases tension with Mexico: Gen. Zachary Taylor advances into Texas to protect new state: July.

1846 United States, with Regular Army of 7,500, declares war on Mexico: May 13.

Oregon boundary dispute with Britain settled, removing possibility of wars on two fronts: June 15.

Zachary Taylor's troops capture Monterey: September 25.

1847 Remaining Mexican forces in California surrender to Capt. John C. Frémont: January 13.

Taylor defeats Mexicans under Santa Anna at Buena Vista: February 22–23.

Main U.S. force, under Gen. Winfield Scott, advances from Vera Cruz towards Mexico City; Mexicans defeated at Cerro Gordo: April 18.

Scott's forces raise U.S. flag in Mexico City: September 14.

1848 Zachary Taylor elected President: November.

1850 President Taylor dies; succeeded by Vice President Millard Fillmore: July 9.

Compromise of 1850, a series of acts to reconcile North-South differences, adopted by Congress: September.

West Point

Henry Brewerton becomes 8th superintendent: August 15.

1852 50th anniversary of the Academy celebrated.

Robert E. Lee becomes 9th superintendent: September 1.

1854 West Point Museum founded.

Course of instruction lengthened from four to five years: August 28.

1855 Old riding hall completed.

John G. Barnard becomes 10th superintendent: March 31.

1856 Richard Delafield becomes 11th superintendent: September 8.

1858 Course of instruction shortened to four years.

1859 Course of instruction again lengthened to five years: April 5.

1860 Winfield Scott gives his "fixed opinion" that West Pointers were the decisive factor in Mexican War.

Davis Commission, headed by Sen. Jefferson Davis, appointed to review curriculum: June.

Academy's prestige underlined by visit in fall of Prince of Wales.

Henry S. Farley of South Carolina, first cadet to leave Academy to join his state forces, resigns: November 19.

1860 to 1861 Of 278 cadets in November 1860, 86 were from South; 65 of these resigned, were dismissed, or were discharged for reasons connected with the impending Civil War.

1861 Course of instruction shortened to four years again.

Pierre G.T. Beauregard becomes 12th superin-

United States

1852 Franklin Pierce elected President: November.

1854 Kansas-Nebraska Act designates area for free or slave settlement; pro-slavery and free-soil groups clash.

Commodore Matthew C. Perry signs friendship treaty with Japan opening ports to United States: March 31.

1856 James Buchanan elected President: November.

1857 Dred Scott Decision widens gap between North and South: March 6.

1858 Abraham Lincoln gains national recognition for anti-slavery views in debates with Stephen Douglas: August-October.

1859 John Brown attacks federal arsenal at Harper's Ferry, Virginia; Brown taken prisoner by Col. Robert E. Lee: October 16–18.

1860 The Henry repeating rifle manufactured by Oliver Winchester.

Abraham Lincoln elected President without winning a Southern state: November 6.

South Carolina secedes from the Union: December 24.

1861 Following secession of ten other states, Confederate States of America elect Jefferson Davis as provisional president: February 9.

tendent: January 23.

Richard Delafield becomes 13th superintendent: January 28.

Alexander H. Bowman becomes 14th superintendent: March 1.

First Class graduates early, May 6; new First Class is graduated and commissioned, June 24.

Confederate Gen. P.G.T. Beauregard opens fire on Fort Sumter, S.C.: April 12.

President Lincoln declares state of insurrection: April 15.

At 1st Battle of Bull Run, Union routed at Manassas Junction, Virginia (July 21); George B. McClellan becomes Union general-in-chief: July 24.

1862 Gatling gun, capable of 350 rounds per minute, patented; adopted by Army, 1866.

Monitor and *Merrimac* clash in first battle between ironclad ships: March 9.

Battle of Shiloh inflicts heavy losses on both sides: April 6–7.

Robert E. Lee becomes commander of South's Army of Northern Virginia: June 1.

Maj. Gen. Henry Halleck replaces McClellan as general-in-chief: July 11.

Inconclusive fighting at Antietam, Md., becomes Union victory when Lee withdraws to Virginia: September 17.

Maj. Gen. Ambrose Burnside's Union army decisively defeated at Fredericksburg, Md.: December 13.

1863 Attempt to defeat Academy's annual appropriation fails in Senate: January.

1863 Lincoln's Emancipation Proclamation declares slaves in Confederate states free: January 1.

South wins costly victory at Chancellorsville; Stonewall Jackson killed: May 2–4.

Battle of Gettysburg, decisive engagement in East, ends with Lee's withdrawal: July 1–3.

Vicksburg, Miss., surrenders to U.S. Grant: July 4.

Draft riots in New York City protest Union methods of raising troops: July 13–16.

Gettysburg cemetery dedicated; Lincoln delivers "Gettysburg Address": November 19.

Grant, now Union commander in the West, drives Confederates from Chattanooga, Tenn.: November 23–25.

1864 Ground for Battle Monument dedicated; Maj. Gen. George B. McClellan speaks: June 15.

Zealous B. Tower becomes 15th superintendent: July 8.

1864 President Lincoln reelected: November.

Given supreme Union command, Lt. Gen. U.S. Grant begins campaign of attrition against Lee; battles of Wilderness, Spotsylvania, and

West Point

George W. Cullum becomes 16th superintendent: September 8.

1865 Tradition of Class Cup, given to parents of first male child born to class member, begun by Class of 1865.

1866 Congressional act permits superintendent and other officers at West Point to be from any service branch; removes Academy from control of Corps of Engineers: July 13.

Thomas G. Pitcher becomes 17th superintendent: August 28.

1868 George W. Cullum's *Biographical Register* published for first time; it excluded West Pointers who resigned to fight for the Confederacy.

Dedication of statue of Maj. Gen. John Sedgwick, killed at Spotsylvania; monument made of cannon captured there: October 21.

1869 Meeting held to organize Association of Graduates: May 22.

1871 Thomas H. Ruger becomes 18th superintendent: September 1.

1876 John M. Schofield becomes 19th superintendent: September 1.

1877 Henry O. Flipper becomes first black cadet to graduate.

United States

Petersburg result: May–June.

Union's William T. Sherman captures Atlanta: September 2.

Sherman's destructive "march to the sea" culminates in fall of Savannah: December 22.

1865 Hampton Roads Conference fails to reach grounds for peace: February 3.

Confederates withdraw from Petersburg and Richmond: April 2.

Grant meets at Appomattox Courthouse, Va., with Lee, who surrenders: April 9.

President Lincoln fatally wounded; succeeded by Vice President Andrew Johnson: April 15.

Jefferson Davis captured: May 10.

1867 South divided into five military districts under Reconstruction: March 2.

Alaska purchased from Russia: April 9.

1868 Ulysses S. Grant elected President: November.

1871 1st Lt. George M. Wheeler begins survey of United States west of 100th meridian.

1872 Grant reelected President: November.

1876 George A. Custer and men of 7th Cavalry massacred at Little Big Horn: June 25–26.

1877 Reconstruction era in South ends; last federal troops withdrawn.

Rutherford B. Hayes declared victor in disputed presidential election of 1876: March 2.

West Point

1881 Oliver O. Howard becomes 20th superintendent: January 21.

1882 Wesley Merritt becomes 21st superintendent: September 1.

1883 Thayer Monument dedicated; address by Maj. Gen. George W. Cullum: June 11.

1884 *Howitzer*, later the official cadet yearbook, first published.

1887 John G. Parke becomes 22nd superintendent: August 28.

1889 John M. Wilson becomes 23rd superintendent: August 26.

1890 Army plays first football game with Navy, losing 24-0: November 29.

1891 Army plays Navy in baseball for first time, winning 4-3.

1893 Cadet Corps erects white tent city at Chicago's World's Columbian Exposition.

Oswald H. Ernst becomes 24th superintendent: March 31.

1897 Battle Monument, designed by Stanford White, dedicated to members of Regular Army killed in action in Civil War: May 31.

1898 First Class graduates early as Spanish-American War begins: April 26.

Albert L. Mills becomes 25th superintendent: August 22.

Arms and seal of the Academy adopted: October 13.

United States

1880 James A. Garfield elected President: November.

1881 Vice President Chester A. Arthur succeeds assassinated Garfield: September 20.

1884 Grover Cleveland elected President: November.

1887 United States receives right to fortify a naval base at Pearl Harbor, Hawaii: January 20.

1888 Benjamin Harrison elected President: November.

1890 Last Indian opposition crushed at Battle of Wounded Knee: December 29.

1892 Former President Cleveland elected: November.

1896 William McKinley elected President: November.

1898 Battleship *Maine* explodes in Havana, Cuba, harbor: February 15.

War against Spain declared: April 25, made effective from April 21.

Admiral Dewey destroys Spanish fleet in Manila Bay: May 1.

Battle of San Juan Hill, Cuba: July 1.

Hawaii annexed: July 7.

Spanish fleet leaves Santiago, Cuba, harbor and is annihilated: July 3.

West Point

1899 Sec. of War Elihu Root praises Academy's contribution to Spanish-American War: "its graduates . . . have more than repaid the cost of the institution since its foundation."

The colors black, gray, and gold are adopted for use in all athletic contests: March 24.

1900 U.S. Senators each given right to appoint a cadet; President's authority to appoint "at large" cadets expanded to thirty.

Lusk Reservoir named for Lt. Col. James L. Lusk.

Roman Catholic Chapel of the Most Holy Trinity completed.

Cullum Memorial Hall, donated by Maj. Gen. George W. Cullum and completed in 1898, is dedicated: June 12.

1901 Congressional act outlaws hazing: March 2.

1902 Centennial of Academy celebrated; President Theodore Roosevelt is guest of honor: June 9–11.

1903 Architectural firm of Cram, Goodhue, and Ferguson wins design competition for extensive building program.

Officers' club completed, designed by McKim, Mead, and White.

1904 Cadet Corps attends St. Louis Exposition.

1906 All classes must take physical training instruction.

Hugh L. Scott becomes 26th superintendent: August 31.

1908 New building program takes shape; North Barracks completed; Administration Building completed in 1909.

Course of instruction lengthened by three months; new cadets required to report in March.

United States

Brig. Gen. Wesley Merritt receives Spanish surrender of Manila: August 14.

Treaty of Paris ends war with Spain: December 10.

1899 Philippine forces under Emilio Aguinaldo revolt against U.S. rule, beginning Philippine Insurrection, 1899–1902: February 4.

1900 U.S. troops help relieve Peking in China's Boxer Rebellion: August 14.

1901 President McKinley, reelected in 1900, assassinated; Vice President Theodore Roosevelt succeeds him: September 14.

Army War College founded: November 27.

1903 Army General Staff Corps established: February 14.

Wright brothers' plane flies at Kittyhawk, N.C.: December 17.

1904 Theodore Roosevelt elected President: November.

1905 President Roosevelt mediates treaty to end Russo-Japanese War: August 9.

1908 William Howard Taft elected President: November.

West Point	United States
1909 Constitution Island donated to West Point.	
1910 Cadet Chapel completed; seats 1,500; has largest church organ in Western Hemisphere. Anthem "The Corps" sung for first time; lyrics had been written for Centennial; music composed 1910: June 12. Thomas H. Barry becomes 27th superintendent: August 31.	
1911 Riding Hall completed. Old Chapel moved to entrance to cemetery. Course of instruction returns to four years.	
1912 Clarence P. Townsley becomes 28th superintendent: August 31.	**1912** Marines land in Nicaragua to secure U.S. interests: August 14. Woodrow Wilson elected President: November.
	1913 U.S. opposition to Mexican leader Victoriano Huerta imperils U.S.-Mexican relations.
1914 Koehler Manual, named for Herman J. Koehler, Master of the Sword, issued; becomes the basis for Army physical training throughout World War I era.	**1914** U.S. forces occupy Vera Cruz, Mexico: April 21. World War I starts in Europe: August 1–4. Panama Canal, built under direction of Col. George W. Goethals, opens: August 15.
1915 Celebrated "class the stars fell on" graduates; members include Dwight D. Eisenhower and Omar N. Bradley: June 12.	**1915** Preparedness Movement, military training for civilians, gains support. Anti-German sentiment increases with sinking of *Lusitania* and loss of U.S. lives: May 7. U.S. troops land and begin military occupation of Haiti: July 29.
1916 Academy's Washington Monument completed. Cadets organize "vigilance committee" to investigate suspected cheating; evolves into Honor Committee to oversee honor system under Superintendent MacArthur. John Biddle becomes 29th superintendent: July 1.	**1916** Raid by Pancho Villa on Columbus, N.M., causes 16 American deaths: March 9. Brig. Gen. John J. Pershing leads punitive expedition into Mexico in pursuit of Villa: March 15. Council of National Defense established to organize national security: August 29. President Woodrow Wilson reelected: November.
1917 Samuel E. Tillman becomes 30th superintendent: June 13. World War I brings accelerated graduations; First Class graduates April 20; Second Class (originally 1918) August 30.	**1917** As war with Germany looms, U.S. force withdraws from Mexico: January–February. United States breaks diplomatic relations with Germany, which had resumed unrestricted submarine warfare, February 1: February 3. United States declares war on Germany: April 6.

214

West Point	United States
	Selective Service Act requires registration for military service: May 18.
	First Liberty Loan drive held: June.
	Espionage Act, followed by Sedition Act (May 16, 1918), passed to protect national security: June 15.
	John J. Pershing, commander of the American Expeditionary Force, promoted to full general: October.
	Parts of 1st Division move to the front in France: October 21.
1918 Original Class of 1919 graduates June 12; Original Classes of 1920 and 1921 graduate November 1; Class of 1921, redesignated Class of 1919, returns to Academy as student officers after armistice.	**1918** President Wilson outlines his plans for peace in Fourteen Points: January 8.
	U.S. troops block German advance at Château-Thierry: June 3–4.
	85,000 Americans fight in 2nd Battle of the Marne: July 18–August 6.
	Over 500,000 A.E.F. troops reduce St. Mihiel Salient: September 12–16.
	About 1,200,000 Americans engage in final campaign, Meuse-Argonne Offensive: September 26–November 11.
	Armistice signed with Germany: November 11.
1919 French Cadet Monument built; presented by cadets of France's L'Ecole Polytechnique.	**1919** Prohibition Amendment (18th) to Constitution, outlawing liquor, ratified: January 29.
Douglas MacArthur becomes 31st superintendent: June 12.	Germany signs Treaty of Versailles: June 28.
	Woman Suffrage Amendment (19th) to Constitution ratified: August 26th.
1920 Intramural athletics for all classes established.	
Superintendent MacArthur changes traditional summer camp by sending cadets to Fort Dix, N.J., for training.	
Revision and modernization of course of instruction begins at direction of MacArthur.	
	1921 Veterans Bureau established as independent agency: August 9.
1922 Fred W. Sladen becomes 32nd superintendent: July 1.	**1922** Washington Armament Conference ends; treaties primarily concern naval arms and warfare: February.

BIBLIOGRAPHY

Ambrose, Stephen E., *Duty, Honor, Country: A History of West Point* (The John Hopkins Press, 1966).

The Association of Graduates U.S.M.A.: (Proceedings, Correspondence, & Records: 1869–1945 and 1945–1951 (United States Military Academy).

Baumer, William H., *West Point: Moulder of Men* (D. Appleton-Century, 1942).

Beard, Charles A. and Mary R., *The Rise of American Civilization* (Macmillan, 1942).

Berman, Bennett and Monbeck, Michael, *West Point: An Illustrated History of the United States Military Academy* (James J. Kery, Ltd., 1978).

Boorstin, Daniel J., *The Americans*, 3 volumes (Random House, 1958, 1965, 1973).

Boroff, David, "West Point, Good Enough?" (*Harpers*, December 1962).

Bradley, Omar N., *A Soldier's Story* (H. Holt and Company, 1951).

Cable, Mary, *American Manners and Morals* (American Heritage Publishing Company, 1969).

Centennial of the United States Military Academy, 2 volumes (United States Military Academy, 1904).

Cullum, George W., *Biographical Register of Officers & Graduates of the U.S. Military Academy* (United States Military Academy, 1891).

Dickens, Charles, *American Notes* (1842; reprinted, Macmillan & Co., Ltd., 1903).

Dupuy, R. Ernest, *Men of West Point* (William Sloane Associates, 1951).

Dupuy, R. Ernest, *Where They Have Trod: The West Point Tradition in American Life* (Frederick A. Stokes Company, 1940).

Freeman, Douglas Southall, *Lee's Lieutenants, A Study in Command* (Charles Scribner's Sons, 1942).

Ganoe, William A., *A History of the U.S. Army* (D. Appleton-Century, 1942).

Guide to West Point and the U.S. Military Academy (D. Van Nostrand, 1867).

Hubbard, Elmer, "The Military Academy and the Education of Officers," *Journal of the Military Service Institution XVI* (January, 1895).

Klaw, Spencer, "West Point, 1978," *American Heritage*, (June/July, 1978).

MacArthur, Douglas, *Reminiscences* (McGraw-Hill, 1964).

Maddox, Robert, "The Grog Mutiny," *American History Illustrated* (December, 1981).

Mahan, Dennis Hart, *Advanced-Guard, Outpost and Detachment Service of Troops, with the Essential Principles of Strategy and Grand Tactics* (Wiley and Putnam, 1847).

Masland, John W., and Rachway, Laurence I., *Soldiers and Scholars: Military Education and National Policy* (Princeton University Press, 1957).

Morison, Samuel Eliot, *The Oxford History of the American People* (Oxford University Press, 1965).

Newhall, Beaumont, *The History of Photography* (Museum of Modern Art, 1978).

Nye, Russell, *The Cultural Life of the New Nation, 1776–1830* (Harper and Company, 1960).

Schaff, Morris, *The Spirit of Old West Point 1858–1862* (Houghton Mifflin, 1907).

Schofield, John McA., *Forty-Six Years in the Army* (The Century Company, 1897).

Sergent, Mary Elizabeth, "Classmates Divided," *American Heritage* (February 1958).

ACKNOWLEDGEMENTS

The author of a book that deals with such a wide range of history as that covered by *Officers and Gentlemen* must be grateful to many people.

The first debt that must be acknowledged is to Stephen Ambrose and his definitive history of West Point, *Duty, Honor, Country* (The Johns Hopkins Press, 1966). Mr. Ambrose's exhaustive research and thoroughly accessible text coordinate and supersede all previous work done on the military academy, and it is to his book that I owe my understanding of the Academy's times of growth and of its fallow periods.

The staff members at the United States Military Academy with whom I worked were consistently cooperative and patient. I would particularly like to thank Robert Schnare, Assistant Librarian for Special Collections, for his interest in this project from its inception and for his careful reading of the completed manuscript.

I would also like to thank Archivists Edward Kass, Joanne Nocton, and Kenneth Rapp of the USMA Archives; Marie Capps, Elaine Eatroff, Pat Dursi, and Judith Sibley of the USMA Library Special Collections; and Michael Hordeski, John Thigpen, Rex Conniff, and Michael Fusco of the AVIT Division, Photographic Production Section.

At the Prints and Photographs Division of the Library of Congress—an invaluable resource for anyone who works with a photographic history—Oliver Jensen, Jerry Kearns, and Leroy Bellamy were professional and helpful, as they always are.

At Fort Sill, Lynda S. Roper had an immediate understanding of the project and assembled a fine selection of photographs for us.

Alexander Sharp Bennet, West Point Class of 1919, was especially helpful in assembling the photographs of the Bennet family that appear in the portfolio, A Military Family, and the background material for the accompanying text. Colonel Bennet's niece, Emilie Bennet Terry Clifford, also contributed information about the family. The collection of Colonel Richard C. Singer gave the author a personalized view of life at the Academy in the era immediately after World War I.

Enid Klass did thorough research in the field by visiting the Bennet and Singer families in San Antonio, Texas.

I would like to thank Harris and Margaretta Barton Colt of The Military Bookman in New York City for their help with this project, as well as for a decade of the most supportive professional and friendly enthusiasm.

At Sleepy Hollow Press, Saverio Procario and James Gullickson were helpful with their good faith and support, both before the project commenced and during the publication process.

I am grateful to Suzanne S. Burke of Sachem Publishing Associates, Inc. for her patience with the details and mechanics of research. Finally, I wish to thank Stephen P. Elliott of Sachem Publishing for his wit and intelligence while working on the project as well as acknowledging my debt to him for first exploring the marvelous cache of photographs at the United States Military Academy. Susan Carter Elliott of Sachem Publishing applied her critical intelligence to the text and her encouragement to my spirit, for which I thank her.

CREDITS

Jacket: Library of Congress
Title Page: Special Collections Division, USMA Library
p. 9, 10, 11, 13: USMA Archives
p. 14–15 (left), 15, 16–17, 18: Special Collections Division, USMA Library
p. 19, 20, 21 (both), 22: USMA Archives
p. 23: US Army Photograph
p. 24, 26, 27, 28: USMA Archives
p. 29, 30, 32–33: Special Collections Division, USMA Library
p. 34: USMA Archives
p. 35: Special Collections Division, USMA Library
p. 37: USMA Archives
p. 38: Library of Congress
p. 39, 40–41: USMA Archives
p. 42, 43: Special Collections Division, USMA Library
p. 44, 45, 46: USMA Archives
p. 47: US Army Photograph
p. 48: Special Collections Division, USMA Library
p. 49, 50–51, 53: USMA Archives
p. 54, 55: Library of Congress
p. 56 (left): US Signal Corps Photograph
p. 56 (right), 57 (both), 58, 60: Library of Congress
p. 61: USMA Archives
p. 62, 63: Library of Congress
p. 64 (left): Special Collections Division, USMA Library
p. 64–65, 66–67: Library of Congress
p. 68: USMA Archives
p. 69 (both): Special Collections Division, USMA Library
p. 70 (both), 71, 72, 73, 74: Library of Congress
p. 75: USMA Archives
p. 76: National Archives
p. 77 (top): Fort Sill Museum
p. 77 (bottom), 79, 80–81, 82 (bottom left): Library of Congress
p. 82–83 (top): US Signal Corps
p. 82–83 (bottom): Library of Congress
p. 85: Special Collections Division, USMA Library
p. 86–87 (both), 88: Library of Congress
p. 89: Special Collections Division, USMA Library
p. 90, 91: Courtesy of Colonel (ret.) Alexander S. Bennet
p. 92–93: USMA Archives
p. 94–95 (top): Library of Congress
p. 94 (bottom): Special Collections Division, USMA Library
p. 95 (bottom): USMA Archives
p. 96–97: Library of Congress
p. 99: University of Texas Institute of Texan Cultures, San Antonio, Texas
p. 100, 101, 102: USMA Archives
p. 102–103: Library of Congress
p. 104 (top), 104–105: Special Collections Division, USMA Library

p. 106–107, 107: USMA Archives
p. 108: Library of Congress
p. 109 (both): USMA Archives
p. 110–111: Library of Congress
p. 112, 113, 114 (both), 115, 116, 117, 118 (both), 118–119, 120 (both), 121 (top): USMA Archives
p. 121 (bottom): Library of Congress
p. 122, 123: USMA Archives
p. 124, 125, 126–127 (top), 126–127 (bottom): Library of Congress
p. 128, 129: USMA Archives
p. 130: Special Collections Division, USMA Library
p. 131, 132–133, 134: USMA Archives
p. 135: Special Collections Division, USMA Library
p. 136, 137, 138–139, 140, 141: USMA Archives
p. 142–143: Library of Congress
p. 144: USMA Archives
p. 145, 146–147 (top), 146 (bottom), 147 (bottom), 148–149, 150–151: Library of Congress
p. 152: USMA Archives
p. 153 (top): Library of Congress
p. 153 (bottom): USMA Archives
p. 154 (top left): Special Collections Division, USMA Library
p. 154–155 (bottom): USMA Archives
p. 155 (top right), 156 (both): Special Collections Division, USMA Library
p. 157 (left): National Archives
p. 157 (center, right): USMA Archives
p. 158, 159, 160: Special Collections Division, USMA Library
p. 160–161, 161: USMA Archives
p. 162, 163: Special Collections Division, USMA Library
p. 164: USMA Archives
p. 165, 166, 167, 168, 169: Special Collections Division, USMA Library
p. 170, 171: Library of Congress
p. 172, 173 (top), 173 (bottom), 174: Fort Sam Houston Museum
p. 175, 176–177: Library of Congress
p. 178–179, 180 (both), 181: USMA Archives
p. 183 (all), 184, 185 (all), 186: Courtesy of Colonel (ret.) Alexander S. Bennet
p. 188–189: Special Collections, USMA Library
p. 190: USMA Archives
p. 191, 192: Special Collections Division, USMA Library
p. 193: USMA Archives
p. 194–195: Library of Congress
p. 195: US Army Photograph
p. 196–197: USMA Archives
p. 198, 199, 200 (top, bottom), 201, 202: Special Collections Division, USMA Library
p. 203: USMA Archives

INDEX

Page number references appearing in italics refer to photographs and captions.

The typeface used in *Officers And Gentlemen* is Zapf International

The paper is Old Forge Velvelith

Composition by Eastern Typesetting Company, S. Windsor, Connecticut

Printing by Aristographics, Inc., New York, New York

Binding by A. Horowitz & Sons, Inc., Fairfield, New Jersey